Self-defence

for women

To my husband,
son and daughter
for all their help

Self-defence
for women

An easy and effective method of self protection suitable for the non-martial artist, using the principles of A.P.A.P. – Awareness – Psychology – Avoidance – Physical

Lavinia Soo-Warr

Published by SILVERDALE BOOKS
An imprint of Bookmart Ltd
Registered number 2372865
Trading as Bookmart Ltd
Blaby Road
Wigston
Leicester LE18 4SE

© 2004 D&S Books Ltd

D&S Books Ltd
Kerswell,
Parkham Ash, Bideford
Devon, England
EX39 5PR

e-mail us at:-
enquiries@dsbooks.fsnet.co.uk

This edition printed 2006

ISBN 10: 1-84509-460-3

ISBN 13: 9-781-84509-460-7

DS0164. Self-Defence for Women

Creative Director: Sarah King
Project editor: Sally MacEachern
Designer: Axis Design Editions
Photographer: Colin Bowling

The system of self-protection A.P.A.P. – Awareness, Psychology, Avoidance, Physical
– is copyright to Lavinia Soo-Warr

Font used within this book: Helvetica

Printed in Thailand

1 3 5 7 9 10 8 6 4 2

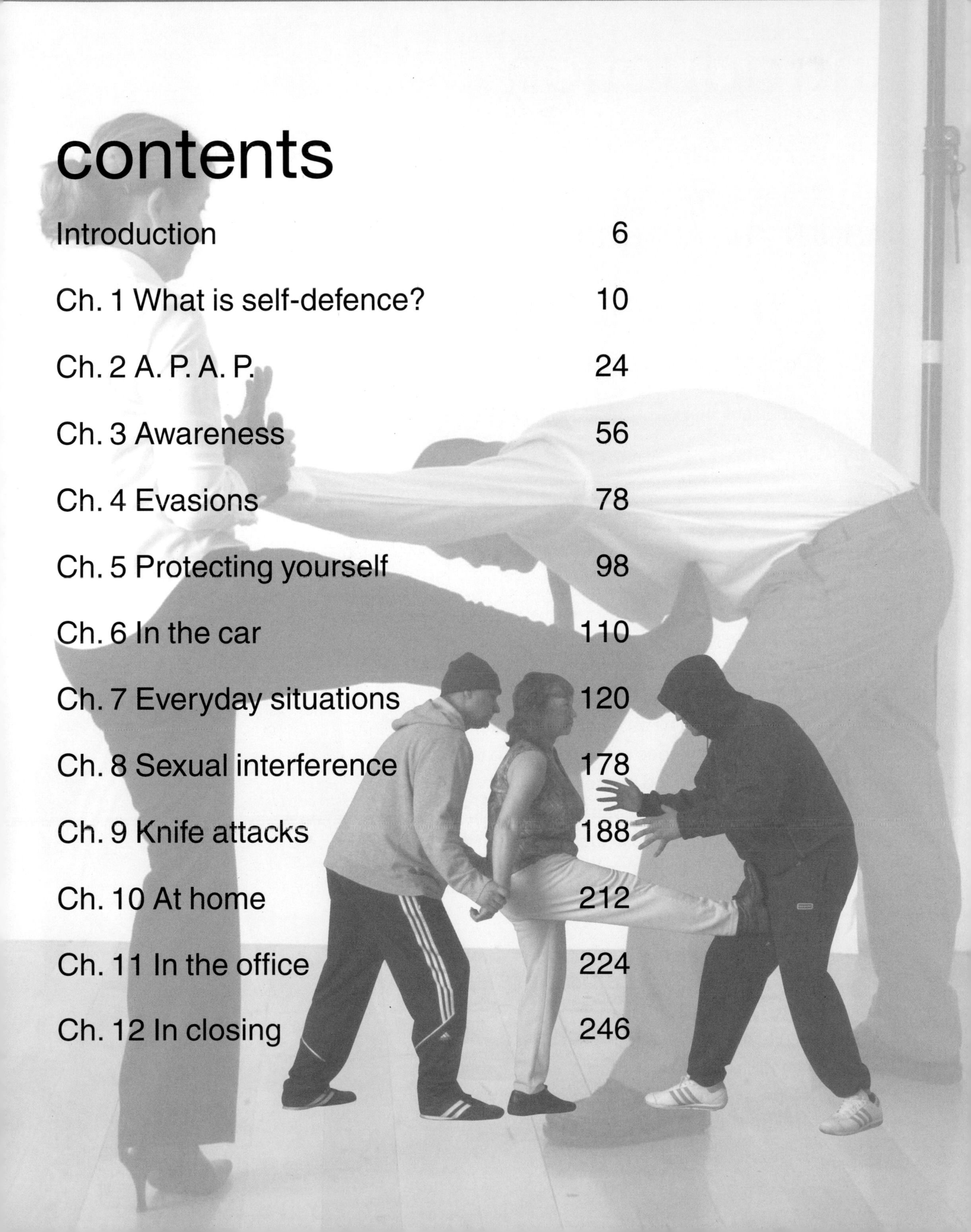

contents

Introduction 6

Ch. 1 What is self-defence? 10

Ch. 2 A. P. A. P. 24

Ch. 3 Awareness 56

Ch. 4 Evasions 78

Ch. 5 Protecting yourself 98

Ch. 6 In the car 110

Ch. 7 Everyday situations 120

Ch. 8 Sexual interference 178

Ch. 9 Knife attacks 188

Ch. 10 At home 212

Ch. 11 In the office 224

Ch. 12 In closing 246

introduction

ABOUT THE AUTHOR

I was born in West Ham, London during May, 1946. My father, Chee Soo (English name Clifford Gibbs) was a half Chinese and half English orphan.

When my father was in his early teens, he used to like playing ball in the local park. On one occasion when he was kicking his ball it hit an elderly gentleman sitting on one of the benches in the park. My father went to apologise and found himself looking at another Chinese person. This was quite a shock, as there were not many Chinese in the area at that time. This chance meeting between my father and businessman Chan Kam Li led to a friendship between the two.

Master Li felt sorry for this young Chinese orphan, so he took him under his wing and taught him his family style of Chinese martial arts.

The Second World War interrupted my father's training, although he used his martial arts to great effect in keeping himself alive during his captivity and ultimate escape in the Burmese jungle.

After the war my father wanted to resume his training, but Master Li had died and so he was unable to continue his Chinese martial arts training. Instead he embarked on the Japanese martial arts of Judo and Aikido, becoming black belt in both arts.

I was just a few months old when my father put me onto the mat and started to teach me rolling break falls. By the time I reached my teens I was training five evenings a week and most weekends. I trained in Judo and Aikido, becoming 1st dan black belt in both. When I was 17 my father decided to return to the Chinese martial arts.

When I was five, I started at the local school, but only stayed for just over a year. My parents then put me into a private school at Leytonstone, where I studied until my family moved from London to Somerset.

This was a huge change in my life, going from a city to the smallest village in the area. There were about ten houses in the village, which had no church, no shop and no pub. The closest shop was about two miles away, and the closest school was a two-mile walk to the bus stop, followed by a 15-mile bus or coach trip to school.

After just three months my family moved to Devon, but again only for a few months. Getting to school was much easier this time with just a two-minute walk and a six-mile bus ride, and there was also a shop in the village.

These moves were difficult in many ways, mainly because the local people were not used to foreigners and had never seen anyone who looked Chinese. I became an object of curiosity. People constantly stared and wanted to touch my face, saying things like, "oh it's warm".

My family's final move was to Dunstable in Bedfordshire, which is where my mother came from. My father once again started up a martial arts club. This became very successful. My father and I not only taught classes but also teacher training sessions, as well as giving seminars and demonstrations all over the country.

The Chinese arts that my father taught were :

- Kung Fu Feng Shou (incorporating kicking techniques), Shuai Chiao Chinese wrestling, two and three man routines, Self-defence, Open Hand forms, Weapon forms

- Chee Shu the art of Locking and Throwing,

- Taijiquan Original Li Style,

- Kai Men Chinese Yoga

I am a qualified instructor in all these arts. My other serious sport interests included horse riding, badminton, netball, and rifle shooting. I also tried Karate, Kendo, archery, baseball, tennis, gymnastics and sword fencing, but only in Kendo did I train long enough to reach the grade of Orange belt.

My husband Peter and I now run the Wu Kung Federation teaching the Chinese martial arts. In 1988 Peter went to study at the Shanghai Physical Institute in China, where he became the first European to achieve an International Wushu Federation Judge's degree. Since then Peter has officiated at all International, European and National Championships. I have been involved with Chinese cultural arts all my life, as has Peter. The knowledge and experience we have gained inspired us to form a business that would incorporate a holistic approach to healthcare, and so the Morningside Health Workshop was born.

chapter 1 What is self-defence?

Self-defence, or self-protection, is exactly that. It is a way of protecting yourself against a person, or persons, who is intent on causing you harm by hurting you or stealing from you.

WHAT IS SELF-DEFENCE?

There are a number of common misconceptions about self-defence, about the teaching of self-defence and about the philosophy behind self-defence. One of the most common is often voiced by women when they ask about learning self-defence. They think they will be taught a martial art, such as Kung Fu, Karate, or Tae Kwon Do. However, noble as these arts are, they are not, in and of

themselves, programmes of self-defence, although many of the physical techniques involved in self-defence have their foundation in those arts. Martial arts are concerned with form, knowledge, ritual, discipline, tradition, culture, exercise and sport. Self-defence is not. Self-defence is concerned with survival.

This technique is from the Kung Fu system of Tan Tui. Self-defence is not a martial art, it's about survival.

Another common statement made by women on self-defence courses is, "… what use is it? [Self-defence] If a big man grabs me I would never be able to get him off …". I will return to this point later, but this feeling of being defenceless is related to another misconception concerning self-defence, which is that it is all about the physical technique at the point of attack. Again this is wrong. Self-defence begins a long time before any attack takes place. The most successful preventative measure you have against an attack is a projected confidence; assailants will rarely tackle someone who appears to be full of confidence, instead they will look for those who appear to be insecure, weak and easily controlled.

When it comes to an actual attack the most successful defence you have is not to be there. That may sound like a flippant response to what is, after all, a very serious matter. But avoidance is always the best defence. In fact, avoidance is one of the central tenets of the programme of self-defence that I have developed over the last 30 years: A.P.A.P. (Awareness, Psychology, Avoidance, Physical). This is the programme that I have outlined in this book.

The most crucial element of self-defence is Awareness. Most people walk through this world completely oblivious to their environment, to who inhabits that environment and, more importantly, to who represents a danger in their environment. This is where the real danger lies. By paying attention to your environment and to those who inhabit it, you can greatly reduce the opportunities that an assailant may have to attack you. You also need to be aware of your own capabilities, your strengths and your weaknesses. In short, you need to have awareness of yourself.

I would like to confront another common misconception at this point. It ties in with the tenet of Awareness. There is a belief, promulgated by the popular press, that the rapist is a psychotic stranger who is going to leap out of the dark. Although this does happen, as the recent case of the M25 rapist who attacked women and young girls in and around Kent

Wherever you are, be aware of your surroundings.

and Essex proves, this type of attack is by far the rarest of sexual assaults. A related belief concerns the victims of these attacks. It is perpetuated by denial: "It won't happen to me; that sort of thing happens to other women".

Here are some statistics from the Rape Crisis Federation of England & Wales:

- 1 in 4 women suffer rape or attempted rape
- 97% of callers to the Crisis Help Lines knew their assailant
- The most common rapists are current and ex-husbands or partners
- Fewer than 7% of callers had reported the incident to the police

As you can see, especially from points two and three, if someone is going to make an attempt at sexual violence towards you it is likely to be someone you know.

The statistics for physical assault/domestic violence demonstrate this even more clearly! Domestic violence is another huge problem faced by women. The Police Federation statistics show that domestic violence accounts for 25% of all reported violent crime. And that is just what is reported; the actual figures are estimated to be far higher. It is a harrowing truth but one that you should know. Ignorance in this field does not lead to bliss.

The second tenet of my self-defence programme is Psychology. There is a whole panoply of psychological states and influences involved in any confrontational, or potentially confrontational, situation. Not only is there your own

As you never know for certain whether anyone in a group could turn out to be an attacker, never leave your drink unguarded. Take it with you or ask a trusted friend to keep an eye on it.

psychological state but also that of the assailant/potential assailant. Sexual assault, domestic violence and even street robbery are all about an assailant asserting control and power over their chosen victim. The tool that an assailant will use to achieve this control is fear. This often engenders panic in the victim rendering them unable to think, or act, clearly and effectively. The more someone panics the easier it is to control their actions. However, if you are able to control your own feelings of panic and react consciously to an attack, thus not surrendering control to the assailant, it can have quite a profound result on the mindset of the assailant. Quite often all you need to do to negate a threat is alter the mindset of the assailant, denying him the ability, or opportunity, to control.

Body language can play a big part here. Many women will often adopt what are known as defensive postures when they are on their own, particularly when walking down the street, or in car parks, etc. This is understandable. You are nervous and unsure and this is reflected in the posture that you adopt. However, this is exactly the sort of body language that someone of a predatory nature will pick up on. Most attackers want easy prey. They don't want to tackle someone who is going to fight back, they want a woman who is compliant and easily controlled, a woman who will quickly acquiesce. By adopting a more confident and assertive profile you are more likely to deter any potential attacker, who will then look for easier prey.

Looking dejected or defensive will make you a tempting target.

The next tenet of the A.P.A.P. programme is Avoidance. Again there is vast range of categories that fall under this heading, far too many to cover in this introduction. That being the case I shall, briefly, look at two examples of avoidance. The first is avoidance of dangerous places. Obviously there are places that cannot be avoided. But, for example, if it is not necessary to walk down a street, on your own, late at night, then don't. Again Awareness comes into this point. A little bit of forethought and assessment of your environment will enable you to make decisions that will keep you safe and avoid potentially dangerous areas. The second is avoidance of dangerous situations. If, for example, an abusive and violent ex-boyfriend/partner/husband comes banging on your door demanding to be let in, your best course of action is to keep the door locked and to phone the police. By keeping that physical barrier between you, you can avoid a direct confrontation and maintain an element of control. However, you would be surprised at the number of women who would answer the door. Thus perpetuating his control. Thus acquiescing to the abuse. That may sound harsh but it is an elemental truth; sometimes people, through their own actions, contribute to their own victimisation.

The final tenet of the programme is the Physical aspect. As you would expect this might involve techniques that have their roots in the martial arts, although that is not always the case. In fact, the most successful and the easiest response to any situation in which you find yourself in danger is to run away, to escape, to evade. That may sound rather prosaic but it really is

Dark places can seem threatening.

the safest course of action. However, it is not always possible to run away. That's where the techniques come in. Remember the point that was raised earlier: "… if a big man grabs me I would never be able to get him off …". There is a simple answer to that: no man, regardless of how big and how strong, is invincible. There are techniques that a woman, no matter how apparently frail she may be, can employ in order to defend herself. All men have vulnerable places – genitals, eyes, throat, ears, kneecaps, shins – that, if struck, especially repeatedly, with force, will render them momentarily incapacitated. The important word there is 'momentarily'. It is this window of opportunity that will enable you to escape. The aim is, after all, to escape, not to stand toe-to-toe and fight a man to submission.

A sentiment that is expressed by many women is their unwillingness to hurt or to cause harm. This may give them a negative attitude towards the physical techniques of self-defence, many of which can result in injury and harm. It is a dilemma that each woman must reconcile for herself. I can but offer you the philosophy and techniques of self-defence; it is up to you whether you ever implement them.

The A.P.A.P. programme of self-defence outlined in this book is for every woman. You do not need to have any experience in, or any particular knowledge of, martial arts. The A.P.A.P. programme, and the techniques contained therein, is designed to be easy to learn and implement. It aims to offer some help, information and guidance to the average woman. More importantly, the A.P.A.P. programme is there to enable women to be proactive in defending themselves.

Be aware of possible confrontation.

The aim of this book is to give you an idea of how to use the principles of A.P.A.P. – Awareness, Psychology, Avoidance and Physical.

AWARENESS

This is very important but is probably the least used. You should always be aware of what is going on around you and, more importantly, aware of what your own body is telling you.

Awareness of your surroundings

Where you are:

- in the street (either walking, on a bus, in a car or taxi)
- working in the office or in any other public building
- on an evening out to the theatre or cinema
- using sport facilities

Be relaxed, but also be aware.

Facilities that can be of use/or useful to you

- What are you carrying that you can use?
- Is there anything around you that can be used?
- Is there anyone close at hand who could help you?

There are usually many items in your bag or briefcase that can be used, but are they easy to get hold of very quickly?

Anything you carry can be used to defend yourself.

What can be used as support for you?

- The most important is the police or a police station. If neither is immediately available, then any other emergency facility such as an ambulance or fire station.
- Any shops, sports centres, or other public buildings.
- Any other facility that is in your immediate vicinity.

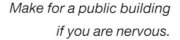

*Make for a public building
if you are nervous.*

Awareness of your situation

What is going on around you?

- Is it crowded?
- Are you on your own?
- Observe what is around you
- But remember most people are just going about their day to day business.

Always listen to what your body is telling you.

What your body is telling you

- If your hair is standing on end, you have goose bumps and are in a cold sweat, your body is telling you something is not right.
- In today's society we seem to have lost the ability to listen to, or even recognise, what our bodies tell us.
- We have to re-educate ourselves to recognise the feelings of our body.
- Always listen to your body because your body is rarely wrong.

Awareness of your own self

- to be calm in temperament
- confident in mannerisms
- completely self-assured in the knowledge of your own capabilities (i.e. strength, ability, fitness etc)

Always walk confidently.

To be verbal

- If the situation warrants it, talk calmly with confidence.
- Or be very loud, trying to attract other people's attention.
- If you need to shout then make your comments short and sharp.

Have the ability to deal with the situation

- Think about the psychology of the situation.
- Think through the situation and decide on the course of action to take.
- If a physical reaction is required, then it will help if you have practised the techniques that you are comfortable with – on both sides.

Unfortunately, in today's society we are apt to live our lives with very little thought about what other people are doing. We tend to think only of ourselves, and our own personal environment. However, we need to be aware that everything about ourselves communicates to others.

Our posture – the way we stand, the way we look, and how we interact with other people – and the way we conduct ourselves all indicate the type of person we are.

As in all situations, whether non-threatening or threatening, 80% of our communications are non-verbal (i.e. body language).

PSYCHOLOGY

Psychology and awareness are very closely linked. Once you have become aware of, or recognise, a situation, you must think through what you need to do, and then decide how best to do it.

You should also be aware that, in any given situation, there are two psychologies in action: yours and the attacker's.

It is very important that you should always remain calm and confident, even if you are shaking in your shoes. To project yourself as being confident can go a long way towards deterrence.

You should never give any indication of weakness – for example, by slouching along with your arms folded or wrapped tightly around yourself, not looking at anyone but keeping your eyes lowered. An attitude such as this indicates defensiveness, insecurity or weakness.

This posture looks defensive and insecure.   *Here she seems confident and alert.*

Do you remember when you were little and you were naughty, how your mother would look at you. That look was always enough to make you quiver in your shoes and send you scampering off to your room.

Such a look can be a very effective deterrent against a possible attacker. In effect, you are saying, "Don't you dare, but if you do, then I am ready for you".

Hopefully, this attitude would also reinforce your confidence and your possible attacker might then leave you alone and look for a much easier target.

An attacker/predator will always look for a victim who displays, or whose demeanour shows, the classic signs of weakness and insecurity, indicating a person who is unable or incapable of defending themselves.

Consider all the relevant details, then make your decision on how to deal with it, keeping your safety or that of your family/friends (if you are not on your own) in mind.

Also take into account that usually you have to assess, decide and act within a very short space of time – in some situations, just a matter of seconds.

Remember that your attacker will be trying to create as much fear in you as he can, as this will give him a great deal of power and control over you.

Your attacker will not give you any time for casual or slow reflection. Remember that he already has a plan of action and will execute that plan as quickly as possible, so that there is less risk to him.

The psychology of the attacker

The psychological elements of each and every attack will be different.

Street robber

If you have been robbed in the street, the chances are that this was an opportunist attack. The robber will have noticed any of the following:

- a purse sitting on top of the shopping
- a purse or wallet sticking out of a back or side pocket
- a bag that is open with the contents in view
- a backpack that is not securely closed or that could be opened easily
- you putting a wallet or purse into one of your pockets
- you seem weak in some way

Over the past few years, a more organised approach to this type of crime has developed. A gang, or gangs, often works together through crowded areas, such as shopping centres, airports, nightclubs, leisure facilities or football matches, relieving victims of their wallets/purses or any other valuable item that they can take easily.

With this type of robbery the sequence of events is usually the same. A few of the gang members will crowd around and may even jostle the victim, while one of the gang actually does the thieving. That gang member will almost immediately pass the purse/wallet onto another gang member, who will pass it on again. In this way, if the first gang member is caught they will not have any incriminating evidence on them.

Many robberies occur shortly after visiting a cash machine.

The opportunist house burglar

This is the most common form of burglary. Burglars will look for open or unlocked windows, open or unlocked doors or any other reasonably easy access to the property, such as the garage, cellar, or sky light. If they think that no one is at home, they may take their time searching for anything that they can dispose of easily, such as the video recorder, hi-fi system, money and jewellery. If the owners of the house are in, the burglars will take whatever they can from unoccupied rooms and leave as quickly and as quietly as possible.

The premeditated burglary

These people (and there are usually more than one) already know what they want, and where they need to go to get it. They have very carefully made their plan of action, deciding how to get into the house and, more importantly, when. They may even know where they have to go to find the item, or items, they want.

An open door is an invitation to a burglar.

They will also have contingency plans for:

- if they are caught on the property
- if they are caught leaving the property
- if they are unable to find the item they want, what alternatives are there

In a premeditated burglary, the burglars will probably be carrying weapons and will be quite prepared to use them if you get in their way.

Has a burglar got in?

Rape

The majority of rapes are premeditated. If the rapist has not already identified a victim, he will be on the lookout for an easy target.

The easy target

Although the rape attack will almost certainly be premeditated, the method will be opportunistic. The mind set of this particular attack is that the rapist knows what he wants or what is going to happen. The rapist will already have a plan worked out and may have picked several different locations; all he will be looking for is a victim. Some of the locations could possibly be:

- short-cuts through wooded or park areas
- lonely alleys or pathways
- behind buildings or walls
- generally quiet areas or times

In some cases, the rapist may already know or have located a victim; he will just be looking for the opportunity. He may well have already followed the victim and knows the route she takes and the times.

Always be extra alert in quiet places.

Premeditated rape

As I have mentioned most rapes are premeditated; it is the way they are executed that makes them different. With a premeditated rape, the rapist has already formed a plan of action and has picked a victim. The location may well be the victim's own home or some other predetermined place.

He will invariably be disguised in some way, usually with a face covering, and will more often than not be carrying a weapon. If the victim is in bed the first thing she will see is the weapon. Inevitably this will cause a great deal of fear, which is the very reaction the rapist wants. The victim may not be able to do anything other than obey the rapist's demands as, with this type of attack, an extreme amount of force may well be used.

However, it is a different type of rapist who accounts for a very large percentage of rape crimes. In these cases, the rapists are known to their victim, as they are usually a partner/husband/ex-partner or ex-husband. The partner usually exerts an extreme amount of control when demanding acquiescence. They will have built this control up over many years, often by the means of physical and mental abuse.

It usually takes a women many years and numerous beatings before she finally thinks to herself, "I have had enough", and then does something about it. Unfortunately, some women do not get to make that choice, but instead die at the hands of the abusive partner.

The problem mostly lies with the fact that the abuse starts off slowly and probably not too badly, with an occasional slap or a thump. In most cases, the abusive partner shows deep remorse for what has happened and invariably promises that it will never happen again. But it always does, and usually within days. In all cases, the abuse always gets progressively worse and more violent.

Someone who looks scared is easily controlled.

No one has to put up with this type of abuse. A woman always has a choice and the best one in this case is to get out of the situation. The choices are:

- Leave him.
- Move out. (If there is nowhere else, go to a refuge centre, as they will give you the mental and physical help and support you may need.)
- Report it to the police. (Any form of physical violence should always be reported to the police.)
- Get help or advice from your doctor, counsellor, refuge centre or anyone else you can trust.

A persistent abuser will often express remorse.

AVOIDANCE

When you become aware that something is not right, you have to decide whether to avoid it or confront it.

With any given situation all information must be evaluated very quickly. Either you need to remove yourself quickly from the situation, so avoiding a direct confrontation, or you can remain within the situation, and take any action that you feel comfortable with, whether verbal or physical.

I have only given two options – avoidance or confrontation – in the knowledge that this is, in effect, simplifying the position you may find yourself in. Avoidance can be effective in numerous situations. Although I cannot begin to cover every situation and how to avoid it, I hope that this book will give you some ways to think about avoidance and how to use it to your advantage.

Remember a lot of situations have been, or can be, defused by simply talking to the attacker in a quiet and calm but positive way. Any verbal remarks should be kept short and sharp (i.e. "No, No").

Never make comments along the lines of, "Please don't hurt me" as your attacker will only hear, or choose to hear, the word "please", and may take it as your agreement to his actions. So keep the wording short.

PHYSICAL

This should be avoided if at all possible. If you have exhausted the previous A.P.A. (Awareness, Psychology, Avoidance) and have failed, then the physical is a must. But it is the absolute last resort, and should only be used for the protection of yourself or your family/friends.

With any situation, fear plays a major role. Try to use or channel that fear into generating the necessary positive response to the situation you face.

Providing the technique you choose is simple or easily performed, and you execute it with ability, speed and determination or intent, the height and weight of your attacker will not necessarily be an important factor.

His size will, or may, cause you a problem, however, if your own mental/psychological state gets in the way. If you allow yourself to think that your attacker's size is too much for you to handle, you will immediately give him the upper hand. By telling or convincing yourself that his size is a problem, and that you may not be able to deal with it, you become passive and give your attacker a much more dominant role.

So you should be mentally convinced that size does not necessarily matter. Remember that your body language will be communicating a great deal about your state of mind.

When teaching some of the techniques used to deal with attackers, I have head comments from women along the lines of the following, " I cannot do that, it might hurt them or me". My response to that is quite simple: if you are unable to do the technique because you do not really want to hurt anyone, and you only have yourself to think of, then that reasoning is perfectly acceptable. But you will have to live with the knowledge and consequences of your inaction.

But if you are not worried about yourself, then consider this: how would you feel if the attack was against your mother, your grandmother or your child? The chances are that you would be quite capable of stepping forward to protect them, and not in the least bit concerned about whether their attacker got hurt or not. This is the feeling you must generate to help yourself. After all, the attacker is not in the least bit interested in you, or your health or whether he hurts you. His only thought is to get what he is after, using whatever force he is prepared to use (which is usually an extreme amount) and then to get away very quickly.

QUESTIONNAIRE

Before continuing, please fill out the questionnaire opposite.

Complete the questionnaire again when you have finished reading the book. Compare your first set of answers to your second, and analyse the effect the information contained in the book has had on your mental attitude towards self-protection. Always remember A.P.A.P.

Think about these questions carefully before ticking the box that you consider to be the correct one. In some instances, you may feel that multiple answers are required.

1. It is very late at night. You've had a good evening with your friends with a lot of laughter and drink, but you find yourself the only one going in the direction of your home. Do you:

☐ Walk with your back to oncoming traffic?
☐ Walk facing oncoming traffic?
☐ Take a poorly lit short-cut?
☐ Take a longer but well lit and busy road?

In a few words explain the choice you made:

....
....
....

2. After your evening out, there are a number of taxis outside the establishment. Do you:

☐ Walk because it saves you money?
☐ Take a taxi regardless of the sex of the driver?
☐ Take a taxi ensuring that the driver is the same sex as yourself?
☐ Take a note of the taxi cab number, and a description of the driver?

3. After an evening out, you find yourself having to walk home on your own. Do you:

☐ Make sure your keys are in your pocket?
☐ Not bother because the keys are just inside your bag/briefcase?
☐ Keep your bag held loosely in your hand?
☐ Keep your bag out of obvious view?
☐ Keep your keys in your hand?
☐ Have your name and address on the keys?

In a few words explain the choice you made:

....
....

4. You know that you are being followed and there is no one around to help. Do you:

- ☐ Turn to face the person and walk past them?
- ☐ Start walking faster?
- ☐ Change the direction in which you are going?
- ☐ Run home?
- ☐ Confront the person?

Explain in a few words why that choice:

....

....

....

5. You are at home. Do you:

- ☐ Leave both back and front doors unlocked?
- ☐ Leave just the back door unlocked?
- ☐ Keep both doors locked?

If you have a chain fixed to the door, do you use it? If not, why not?

....

....

....

6 When leaving your home, do you:

- ☐ Check to be sure all windows are shut and locked?
- ☐ Just check that the windows are shut?
- ☐ Just single-lock the back and front doors?
- ☐ Double-lock the back and front doors?

If you have an alarm fitted, do you:

- [ ] Use it every time you leave the house?
- [ ] Use it occasionally?
- [ ] Use it when you remember?
- [ ] Never bother with it?
- [ ] Not use it because you do not understand how it works?

7. You are travelling though a busy city centre in your car. At some point you will have to stop at traffic lights or a pedestrian crossing. Do you:

- [ ] Keep your bag/briefcase on the seat with doors unlocked?
- [ ] Keep your bag/briefcase on the seat with the passenger door locked?
- [ ] Keep your bag/briefcase on the seat with all doors locked?
- [ ] Have your windows open and doors unlocked?
- [ ] Have your windows shut with doors locked?
- [ ] Hide your bag/briefcase under the seat?
- [ ] Do you just sit idling away the time, wishing to get out of traffic and not paying attention to the activity around you?
- [ ] Do you stay relaxed but alert, on the lookout for possible trouble?
- [ ] Do you read a paper or make a telephone call while waiting?

8. You are travelling alone on the motorway and you break down. Do you:

- [ ] Try to coax the car to the nearest call box?
- [ ] Leave the car and walk to the nearest call box?
- [ ] Stay with your car and hope someone will stop and help?
- [ ] Try to flag someone down to help you?

You can't see a call box, so you must walk to find one. Do you walk facing traffic, or with your back to traffic? Why did you make that choice?

....

....

9. You are out walking alone and you find yourself in a situation that makes you feel uncomfortable. All you have with you is your bag/briefcase and its contents. What is in the bag? Can it be used for protection?

- ☐ Keys
- ☐ Wallet
- ☐ Brush/comb
- ☐ Umbrella
- ☐ Perfume/hairspray
- ☐ Pen
- ☐ Credit card

How heavy is your bag? Could it be used for protection? Please explain your answer.

....
....
....

10. In your opinion, what is the best attribute for self-protection?

- ☐ Confidence
- ☐ The way you walk
- ☐ How you conduct yourself
- ☐ Attitude
- ☐ Acting shy or slouching
- ☐ Standing upright and positive
- ☐ Style of dress

Why did you make the choices you made?

....
....
....

When answering questions like these we invariably know which answers are correct. However, you are not trying to pass an examination, so answer them carefully and honestly. Are your answers a true reflection of your actions? If you have experienced any of the situations, how did you react at the time? And how would you react now with the benefit of hindsight?

When you have read the book return to the questionnaire. Again answer the questions honestly – only you will know which choices you would make in those situations.

Now compare the two questionnaires and think about the differences. Are you more aware of possible dangers? Do you feel more prepared if something should happen? Do you feel that if you practise the techniques and follow the A.P.A.P. system you will be able to handle those situations, and others like them, with greater confidence?

Awareness of your immediate environment is one of the most important aspects of your life, and of self-defence, but it is one that most of us do not use to its full extent.

In all forms of self-protection, the very first step is awareness. This is followed very closely by psychology and avoidance. If all else fails, the final stage is the physical.

AWARENESS – THIS INCLUDES:

- awareness of what you can use as support
- awareness of your surroundings
- awareness of your situation
- awareness of your own ability

Be aware of your surroundings.

Have you ever walked into a room and had any, or all, of the following 'symptoms'?

- Cold shivers down your back.
- Hair feels like it is standing on end.
- A very oppressive feeling.
- A feeling that something is not right.
- A feeling as if something is crawling over your skin.

I am sure we have all experienced something like this at some time, but what do we do about it? Your own body is telling you that something is not right.

You have two options that will require immediate action.
1. Stay in the room and confront the problem.
2. Turn and leave, so avoiding whatever may happen.

Since the beginning of time we have had an in-built survival unit that most people now know as "fight or flight". However, in today's urban society the majority of people have lost the ability to recognise what their body is telling them, or they choose to ignore it. We go about our day-to-day life with the misguided attitude that if we ignore the problem or situation, it will either go away or not affect us. Unfortunately, this is seldom the case.

If you are uncomfortable or fearful, your demeanour will reveal your feelings unless you make a deliberate effort to look confident.

Personal experience

Awareness means recognising the feeling that something is not right. One of my own personal experiences comes to mind.

I had left work with about 50 to 60 other people, all walking up a not very steep but long road. People were walking on both sides of the road (doing what people do when they have just finished work). I suddenly had a very strong feeling that someone had singled me out as a target.

I knew quite a few of the people around me. I turned and spotted a single male walking on the other side of the road about 50 yards away from me.

I could not understand why, with all the other people around, this person had singled me out. More importantly I couldn't imagine what he had in mind. Or, why I knew that he was focussed on me.

I prepared myself for whatever was going to happen. I walked closer to the wall, which luckily ran for about 200 yards. I moved my bag to the inside between the wall and my body. And then carried on walking, I hoped nonchalantly, down the road.

When the man finally caught up with me (I will admit to an enormous sense of relief), he said, "Hello, you're Peter's wife aren't you, how is he?" After talking for a few minutes, he turned into a side road and walked away, and I carried on to my mother's house.

Question: what did I do when I became aware that the man was getting close to me, and how did I know it was me? Here is my answer to this situation, along with the reasons for my actions.

It was the type of feeling that you get when someone behind you is looking at you. You can feel or sense it, and invariably you are able to locate that person straight away. You have no need to scan faces, you just seem to know instinctively which person is looking at you.

I moved closer to the wall so that I controlled the area of the attack, if there had been one. I also ran through my mind several situations and how to deal with them, so that if anything did happen I was not caught unprepared.

I thought through a bag snatch, a physical assault, either armed (with a knife or stick) or unarmed (open hand or fist) and even rape (although this was unlikely with so many people around).

I moved my bag into the small gap between my body and the wall. If a bag snatch was intended this action would make it a lot more difficult, and it also left just one side of my body vulnerable. I again ran through various situations for the exposed side of my body. I did not panic. I remained confident and aware of the changing terrain. I had chosen roughly the area where I thought the attack (had there been one) would happen. I felt in control of the situation and as prepared as I could be, which gave me a great deal of confidence.

How I used A.P.A.P.

AWARENESS
- of the feeling of being targeted
- of the surroundings (i.e. the wall, the people around me)

PSYCHOLOGY
- Mentally prepared myself by running through various attacks (bag snatch, physical assault, rape) and then considering what course of action would be required for each type of attack.
- Remained upright and alert.

AVOIDANCE
- This would have been quite difficult as I could not have avoided the situation. Only with the knowledge of hindsight could I have affected the outcome (i.e. by leaving work earlier or later).
- Avoided the feeling of fear or panic.
- Avoided being a victim.

PHYSICAL
- Thankfully I did not need to use any physical response, although I was prepared and ready to retaliate.

Most attackers have a plan in mind; all they need is the opportunity. The majority of people go about their day-to-day lives not thinking about self-protection. If they are confronted with an unpleasant situation they are totally unprepared.

If you allow fear to gain the upper hand,
you will look and react like a victim.

Most women have never been touched or manhandled by a male outside their circle of family and friends or by a stranger. So when a stranger, or someone whom they do not associate with this type of behaviour, attacks them, their brain just cannot come to terms with what is happening.

The classic symptoms of this are that you freeze, you cannot think straight, you cannot move, you are unable to do anything to help yourself and, in many cases, do not or cannot even scream.

Most boys or men do not react like this because, from an early age, they play rough and tumble games and sport with lots of body contact. So, if someone grabs, punches or throws objects at them, it is not a problem. Their brains have become accustomed or acclimatised to such actions and will respond quickly and almost automatically.

Unfortunately, it is now recognised that a large percentage of attacks are by someone that we know and trust. As a result, we are mentally unable to cope with such an attack as we struggle to deal with the fact that this person whom we know and trust is abusing that position of trust. The emotions that we feel go from shock to absolute disbelief and, possibly, a feeling of degradation. And so, instead of dealing with the attack, we freeze.

Remember that this is exactly the reaction our attacker is wanting or looking for, and by the time we have recovered enough to think, the attack may well be over.

You must overcome this initial reaction – and very quickly – if you are going to protect yourself by defending or retaliating. The longer that you stay passive, the harder it is to mentally deal with or react to the situation.

SITUATION: Being followed

Question: Have you ever thought that you were being followed? What do you do?

The usual reaction is either to become very frightened or to be in a state of shock. As a result, you cannot think straight and probably run, hoping to escape, or to go directly home. Neither of these reactions are very good for several reasons.

By running, you have given the follower immediate confidence as he now knows that you are panicking and unable to think straight. He now has power over you, which will give him even more confidence. This has become a game of hunter and hunted for him.

By going straight home you have led him to the one place you would rather he did not know about. If he is unable to attack you this time, he now knows exactly where you live and can afford to wait for another occasion.

What you must decide before I give you some options is the following:

1. Are you sure that someone is following you?
2. Are your surroundings able to offer you support?
3. Are you close to a police station, or any other public building, such as a fire or ambulance station?

Being followed can be very scary, but try to remain upright and outwardly calm and confident.

Options

1. Ways of checking that you are being followed.

- Use shop windows as mirrors to see who is behind or to the side of you, without making it obvious. If the window is at an angle this might give you a wider view behind you. You might need to stop and look into several shop windows before you can be sure.
- If you are still unsure, you could go into a shop, taking time to watch the doors. If you are in a clothes shop, take articles of clothing into the changing rooms (again look around before you go in) and stay as long as you feel is necessary. On leaving the changing rooms, again take time to look around. If possible, go out of a different door from the one you used to come in.
- Continually look around you. If a face starts to come into view repeatedly, then this could possibly be the person.

The action of the follower is to observe, but they also try not to be obvious. If you turn quickly to look at them, it is likely that they will look away suddenly – into a shop window, pretending to read a newspaper or just trying to appear like another casual pedestrian.

2. Stay in well-lit, populated places. Never ever go into a lonely, quiet area, even if it means taking a long detour or even just walking in a large circle.

Use a shop window as a mirror.

3. If you can, ring a member of your family to come and collect you, or take a taxi.

4. Take any measure you feel is right for the situation you are in.

5. If you are being followed never, never walk directly home.

6. If possible always go to a police station or find a police officer or someone else in authority (i.e. ambulance station, fire station). If any of those are immediately unavailable, go to any other public place, such as a coffee house, a pub, or a shop.

7. Try to build up a full description of the follower so that when you are with the police you can give them as much information as possible.

Personal experience

My daughter experienced a flasher. This was what happened.

> My daughter and her friend were driving home from a nightclub late one night, when a man in a long coat jumped out in front of the car, opened his coat and flashed at them.
>
> After the initial shock, she did the right thing by driving straight to the police station and reporting it. The officer asked her for a description. She told him about the coat and that the man was wearing a suspender belt and stockings and nothing else. '
>
> "Good," said the officer "but can you give a description?" "Yes" she said, "he was wearing a coat, suspender belt and stockings and nothing else".
>
> Unfortunately that was all my daughter and her friend could remember – the coat, the suspender belt and stockings and nothing else.
>
> This, I understand, caused the police quite a lot of amusement, but gave them very little information that could help them to track down the flasher, such as height, build, colour of hair, facial features or any distinguishing marks other than the obvious!

Always try to muster the presence of mind to notice key details, so that the police have as much information as possible to aid them with their work.

If you should find yourself in a quiet/lonely place you could try the following: stop, look into your bag/briefcase pretending to search for something but listening for footsteps. If they stop when you do, don't panic.

If you are carrying a mobile phone, either call the police for help or a family member/friend to come and pick you up. If you are unable to do this and your surroundings (i.e. public building that you could go into) do not offer you any help, then try the following action.

Turn around, and walk back towards your follower. Make sure that your posture is upright and confident. Look at him but don't stare, and take in as much information about him as possible.

Make sure that your posture is upright and confident.

Once you have looked at him, it is very important that you do not then look down. This is a submissive gesture, and will give him a lot more confidence.

Keep walking, preferably back into a well-lit, populated area.

If you still feel that he is behind you, repeat your actions. Turn around and walk back the way you came, again looking at him. If you feel that it is necessary, look at him for a slightly longer period, but again do not look down or lower your eyes. Remain upright and confident.

If you are positive that he is following you, and if the situation is right and only if you feel confident enough to deal with a possible reaction from him, say to him, "Can I help you? Are you lost?"

Keep several feet away from him, giving yourself distance if he should try something. Remember, be prepared for an attack from him, whether verbal or physical.

Only do this if there is no other easier option available to you, and if you are confident that you have the ability to deal with whatever situation may arise from your action.

- If possible, walk close to the wall, house, etc. But be aware of any alleys and dark pathways.
- Keep your bag/briefcase between you and the wall, house, etc.
- Keep your keys in your pocket.
- Never put your address or telephone number on the keys.
- Walk upright in a confident posture.
- Always keep a situation in mind and run through what you can do to protect yourself.
- Change the situation as your surroundings change.
- Don't become paranoid about things. Remember that most people are going about their day-to-day business just as you are.

AWARENESS

- of the feeling that you have been targeted
- of the people around you
- of the one person who has singled you out
- of your immediate surroundings

PSYCHOLOGY

- to evaluate the situation
- to assess what your surroundings can offer in the way of protection or support
- to remain calm and confident

AVOIDANCE

- by staying in a well-lit area
- by staying in a populated area
- by calling for help (from police, family, friends or a taxi)
- by avoiding being a victim

PHYSICAL

- Be prepared with several situations and ways of dealing with them. Adjust your response to changes in the situation.
- If a physical response is required then carry it out with confidence and intent.

SITUATION: Being stalked

This type of harassment is, or can be, very distressing and unnerving. The thought of being followed, of your every movement being watched, of every place you visit being checked, and every telephone conversation being monitored (possibly) can be very unpleasant.

If you are being stalked, or think that you may be, you must establish a record of events, from the very first time you became aware of a person just always being there and watching you or trying to contact you. The record must include dates, times, places and any of the stalker's personal details , such as clothing or any distinguishing features. If possible make a pictorial record as well (i.e. a video or photos, preferably with the date and time imprinted onto each picture or frame).

This record needs to be as complete and comprehensive as you can make it. The reason is that when you go to the police to report it, they can immediately see that this has been going on for a while and is not just a one-off or isolated case.

Another point to keep in mind, is that it is not advisable to talk to, or acknowledge, the stalker in any way. They may take or construe this as encouragement for continuing their actions.

Establish a record of events.

chapter 4 Evasions

One of the first techniques to learn is evasion. The simplest footwork for this is called the box step. It forms the basis for several basic self-defence techniques.

The idea behind these steps is to get you used to moving away from the centre line, or the line of attack.

Mark out on the floor the shape of a square approximately shoulder width. This can be done by measuring across your front or back from the point of one shoulder to the point of the other shoulder.

This is your measurement for the sides of the square.

line of attack

BOX STEP PRACTICE – one side

1. Now move your LF to C3.   **2.** Then move your RF to C1.

Start by placing your right foot (RF) on corner 2 (C2) and your left foot (LF) on corner 1 (C1).

3. Move back to your original position by placing your RF on C2.

4. Now move your LF to C1.

Ensure that when you move, your whole body moves as one unit.
Do not lean your body in any direction, but remain upright and relaxed.

BOX STEP PRACTICE – other side

During this particular exercise you face the centre of the square all the time, close to the line of attack. Practise this movement until you are completely comfortable with it, and you are moving your entire body as a single unit.

1. To practise the other side, move your RF to C4.

2. Move your LF to C2.

Imagine that your hips and shoulders are locked together, so that if your shoulder turns one inch your hips also turn one inch, preferably in the same direction.

After learning these basic steps, start the exercises on the following pages.

3. Now go back again, this time moving your LF to C1.

4. Followed by your RF to C2.

SINGLE BLOCK AND PUNCH

1. At the level of your hip, form your left hand into a fist with the little finger edge touching your hip.

2. Bring your left fist to the centre line of your body, at approximately waist height.

When your fist is almost touching the chin, move the arm away from the body, again turning the fist until the thumb knuckle is pointing to the right. Tighten the muscles in the arm, so that the arm is strong

3. Bring your fist up the centre line of your body towards your chin.

4. Slowly turn your fist until the thumb knuckle is facing towards your body and the little finger is facing away from your body. Keep the elbow down near the waist.

and does not give if some one pushes against it. Your fist should now be approximately 4 to 6 inches away from your temple, with the elbow approximately 12 inches from your centre line.

As the fist moves away from the body, the right hand (either open hand or fist) simultaneously moves out from the body at shoulder height (into either a punch or an open-hand strike). Do not lock the elbow. Try to coordinate the left and right hands so that they work together.

Practise this movement on both sides, until you are completely comfortable with it.

You may find that you need to make slight changes in the distances to suit your personal build. This also applies to the box steps and the block and punch techniques.

Allow the arm and fist to be relaxed until you almost reach the chin and then strengthen the forearm and fist, so that when you take the arm away from the body it is very strong and does not 'give' if someone should push on the forearm.

Once you are comfortable with this movement, then start to incorporate both the left and right fist movements with the box steps.

If possible, start to work with someone such as your brother, your husband or a friend, but make sure that they realise you are doing the exercises to help you against an attacker and not to use against them.

All too often men do not like to give in to a woman, and this can make training very difficult. If you find that the person you have chosen is making training difficult, try someone else. It is for your own protection that you are learning these movements, not to pander to the other person's ego trip!

When you learn any self-protection movement, always do it on both sides and then repeat it until the movement comes naturally and you do not have to think about it.

STEPPING BACK AND DOUBLE BLOCK – one corner

In some situations you will need to put distance between you and your attacker. This can be done using the same principle as the box steps. But instead of moving into your opponent you move away. However, you will still be facing the line of attack.

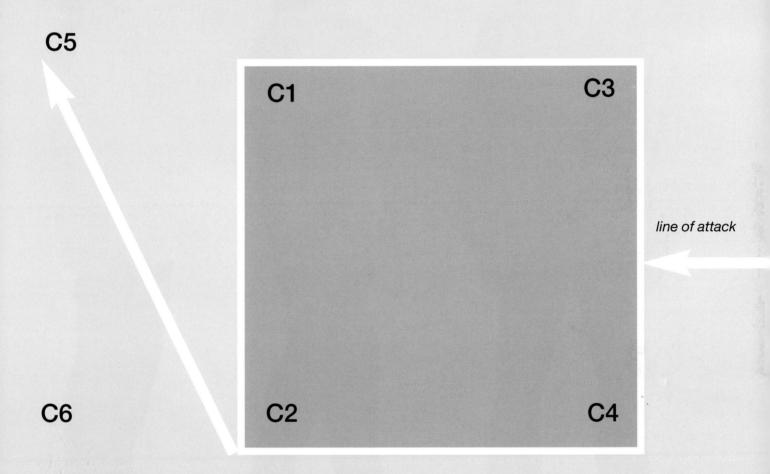

1.

2. Start with your LF on C1 and your RF on C2.

3. Step back with the RF to C5.

4. Adjust the LF, but let it remain on C1.

5. Turn LF 90 degrees but remain on C1. Move RF to C2, back to the start position.

STEPPING BACK AND DOUBLE BLOCK – other corner

This technique can also be done to the other corner of the square. You should repeat it on the opposite side.

1.

2. Start with the LF on C1 and the RF on C2.

3. Move the LF to C6.

4. Adjust the RF, but let it remain on C2.

5. Turn the RF 90 degrees but remain on C2. Move the LF back to C1.

DOUBLE HAND/ARM BLOCK TECHNIQUE

You may also want to practise another defensive movement with your hands. The idea behind this movement is that if something hits your forearms, your fists will not come back and hit you in the face.

1. Make both hands into fists at waist height.

2. Bring both hands to your centre line.

3. Bring both fists up your centre line until they reach your chin. Make sure that the distance between your fists and your elbows is the same.

Once you have the idea of this movement, incorporate it with the foot movements, again making sure you work on all the different angles. The reason for working on different angles is that if you only practise on one side and you get attacked on the other, you can not say, "er, just a minute, but can you attack me on the other side, as I can not defend myself on this side". So, always practise on both sides and with different angles.

4. Turn the fists so that the little finger edge is away from your face.

5. At the same time, tense all the muscles in your arms.

All of these movements must become automatic, like driving a car. When you're driving, you don't think about what gear you are in, when to change gears, or when to signal —you do everything automatically. This must be the same with self-protection. If you have to stop and think about the attack and the counter movements, the chances are that it will be too late.

chapter 5

Protecting yourself

Many everyday items can be used as aids in protecting you from an attacker. Make a mental note of what you are carrying and of the objects around you.

If the first three tenets of A.P.A.P. (awareness, psychology and avoidance) have failed, the last resort is the physical. I have mentioned a few situations that would warrant a physical reaction, and so here are a few techniques that can be useful when you find yourself in those or other situations.

You will want to be prepared with more than just one technique. It does not matter how good you are at doing that technique, you cannot always rely on it working in every situation, or being appropriate for that situation.

Remember that fear can be used in a very positive and powerful way. Rather than just freezing and being unable act, use the fear reaction to generate a response. Go from shock ("Why me?") to anger ("How dare he do that!") to action ("You will not do that".).

As with any emotional effect, this can make you far more powerful/stronger than normal, and more determined not to be taken advantage of.

With any of the situations mentioned, there will almost certainly be a fear response. The attacker will always try to provoke this reaction, as it will give him a greater sense of power over you.

Using everyday items

Handbag

The majority of women carry a handbag, shoulder bag or shopping bag, and usually the bag is quite heavy as everything is put into it.

Check what you are carrying in your bag, and think about which items could be useful if you needed to protect yourself.

The bag itself can be used:

- to deflect or ward off a strike
- to push into the face of your attacker
- to hit your attacker

If the bag is quite heavy, it can be a very effective tool.

Sprays

Spray deodorants, bodyspray, perfume or hair spray can be very effective if sprayed into your attacker's face. They very often make the eyes sting and water, temporarily blinding your attacker, and giving you valuable seconds to get away.

Papers

Newspapers or magazines, if rolled up, can be used very
effectively to deflect a strike or as a weapon in a counter strike.

Keys

Keys or credit/debit cards can be used for striking out, mostly in a slashing movement. They can only be used effectively at close quarters.

Hair brushes and combs

Brushes and combs (especially metal ones) can be very effective in defensive actions or for use in counter-attacking techniques. Again they would be for use at close quarters only.

Umbrella

Umbrellas, whether the long ones with a point or the fold-up
ones, are very good for defensive actions, blocking techniques
or even counter-striking techniques.

Lighters or cigarettes

If you have been grabbed, a lighter can be used effectively to burn your attacker, or a lit cigarette can be pressed onto any exposed skin. This will cause the attacker to release his grip and allow you time to get away.

So, numerous articles within your handbag can be used very effectively, given some thought. Even your shoes can be used for striking or kicking.

The great advantage of using everyday items is that it is perfectly legal for you to carry them. Many countries allow people to carry protective weapons, but in the United Kingdom it is illegal and you can get into serious trouble if you are caught carrying weapons or using them to protect yourself.

Personal experience

On a visit to the United States, I was asked to give a private lesson to a woman whose job was to help abused children. For the sake of this story I will call her Miss A.

I was told that she had a few protection issues she wanted to go over. This I agreed to do. On meeting Miss A I found her to be small and petite, although she had an enormous amount of presence.

After our initial introductions, I asked her what her main and then minor protection concerns were, and we dealt with them in order of priority. Miss A's main concern was that when she arrived at her home, she had her back to the world while she unlocked her front door. She was afraid that someone could attack her from behind.

We ran through several different situations, and I adapted some of the defensive techniques to allow for her stature. They included some of the techniques in this book.

I then asked her what she would normally carry on her during her working day, and she gave me her handbag. I know most women's handbags are heavy, but this bag was exceptionally heavy.

I proceeded to show her different techniques for using the handbag not just for defensive moves but also for attacking ones. We trained for about two hours with me swinging this bag about as I showed her different techniques, incorporating deflection, evasions and counter-attacking movements. I then passed the bag back to her so she could also practise the techniques that I had shown her.

At the end of the session, I talked through with her what we had done during the lesson and asked if she had any questions or problems with anything that I had shown her.

> Never take it for granted that there are only nice or safe things in a bag.

Before we finished, my curiosity got the better of me and I mentioned the weight of the bag. Miss A smiled at me sweetly, opened her bag and handed me a loaded pistol.

I admit I was a bit shocked, but I had enough presence of mind to check that the safety catch was on, which thankfully it was.

My next question was, "Why do you need self-protection lessons when you carry a gun?" "Well", she said, "I have to carry the gun because of my job, but as it is usually in my handbag I might not have time to get the thing out if I needed it". She wanted the assurance of being able to deal with a situation without using the gun. The gun was her very last resort.

As we in the United Kingdom do not generally have a gun culture, I had not even given a thought to the possibility that she would be carrying a gun.

So this was a very good lesson for me. You never know what a women carries in her bag. Never take it for granted that there are only nice or safe things in the bag.

As I did.

chapter 6 **in the car**

When we are in a car we tend to think of it as our own safe, personal space, and we do not stay alert or expect an attack of any sort.

When you travel on your own, there is always the possibility that something unexpected will happen, such as a breakdown, a flat tyre, 'road rage' or an accident. In addition, a dangerous situation may arise while you are waiting for help, or while you are going to get help.

Check oil, water and tyre pressure before setting out.

Here are some things to keep in mind when you are on a motorway alone:

If you have been able to plan your journey, then ensure that the car has been serviced, or at least checked. Check that the water and oil are at the correct levels and that each tyre is at the correct pressure, including the spare tyre, which people usually forget all about.

If you have a problem with the car, always get off the main carriageway and onto the hard shoulder, or into a layby.

If possible, drive or coast until you locate an emergency phone and stop there. Park as far from the main carriageway as possible.

The majority of people now carry a mobile phone, so finding an emergency phone may not be an issue. If you do not own a mobile phone, see if you can borrow one for the journey. But remember that you may be in a dead spot for reception, so don't absolutely rely on it.

Once you have made your emergency phone call, stay on the passenger side of the car. If there is a barrier on the passenger side, step over it and wait for the rescue vehicle or police.

When you first contact the rescue services, be sure you tell them that you are a female and alone. All rescue services now give priority to women in this position, so you should not have to wait too long before they arrive.

If you have a mobile phone, finding an emergency phone will not be an issue.

If you see anyone other than rescue services or police, and you feel they may be threatening to you, get back into the car on the passenger side, lock all the doors and close the windows. Keep the doors locked until the rescue service arrives. Make sure you get a description of the person, as well as their car and their vehicle registration number.

If you are close to a service station, try to coax the car into the service station area. If this is not possible, leave the car, ensuring that any belongings are locked in the boot and that nothing is left visible. Lock the car securely, and walk to the service station keeping as far from the road as possible.

If you know that you are going on a long journey, plan your route in advance. If you are a member of a motoring association check with them to find out if there are road works and adjust your journey accordingly. If you do not belong to an organisation, choose one that you know about. Allow ample time for your journey.

Make sure someone (either a family member or a friend) knows the route you will be taking. If you have to take a detour, contact that person as soon as you can and inform them of the detour.

If you do not have a mobile phone, try to borrow one or hire one. Some emergency services hire mobile phones.

If you are unable to get hold of a mobile, and you are worried about the journey, arrange to ring a member of your family or a friend on a fairly regular basis – preferably about once an hour.

If you are very concerned about travelling on your own, see if a family member or a friend can accompany you.

Here are some things to keep in mind when travelling through a city or town centre:

- Keep all doors locked and keep your windows shut – even when it is hot!
- Keep the sun roof closed.
- Keep all personal belongings out of sight, either in the boot or under the seat.
- Stay relaxed but alert for anything that may happen.
- While driving, if possible, allow space in front of you. Try not to get boxed in.
- Lock the doors immediately you get into the car. If the doors are not locked, someone could get into the passenger seat, possibly with a weapon, and force you to drive to an out-of-the-way place where they can take further action.
- If you have your bag, shopping bag or briefcase on the seat and the doors are unlocked or the windows open, they can easily be grabbed out of the car.

Unfortunately, unsavoury characters are always on the lookout for the unwary. They are very quick to spot a victim, and even quicker in taking action, so you should always be aware of what is going on around you.

REMEMBER A.P.A.P.

AWARENESS
- of where you are
- of who is either near or around you
- of what, if any, possessions are in view
- of the weather – a snatch from the car in good weather because you have the windows open, or in bad weather because you may not notice someone lurking in the rain

PSYCHOLOGY
- Think about your safety by locking car doors.
- Try not to be boxed in. If at all possible allow room to manoeuvre.
- Leave nothing in view to tempt an opportunist.

AVOIDANCE
- by looking around your car, thinking about what an attacker might be looking for, and then changing that situation
- by knowing the route you will be taking and, if possible, avoiding any known bad or rough areas

PHYSICAL
- If someone tries to grab items through the window, push or hit his arm to the closest point of the window frame.

TECHNIQUE

1. An opportunist makes a grab for your handbag through the open car window.

2. Push the attacker's arm against the window frame.

chapter 7 everyday situations

In this next section
I have analysed different
situations that you may
encounter and suggested
ways of dealing with them.

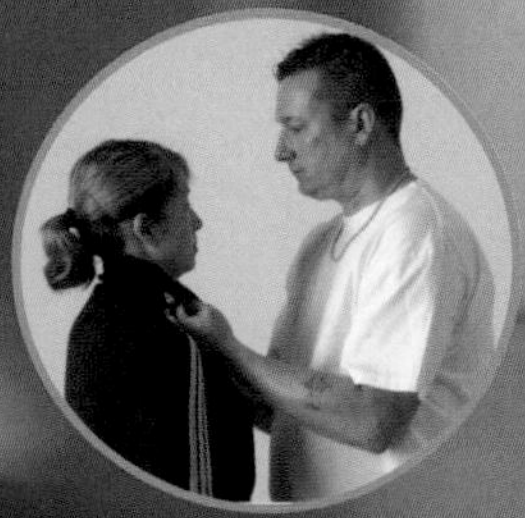

If you are being followed or stalked, you may not be aware of the situation for some time because the person concerned never comes into your personal space. But in this section we look at self-defence techniques you can use if your attacker actually comes so close that he is, as the saying goes, 'in your face'.

If someone actually grabs hold of you it can be extremely frightening. Your legs may feel like jelly and your heart may start pounding in agitation. But, as before, you must control your fear before you can put any of the following techniques into action. You will not be able to act effectively and strongly unless you have yourself under control first.

SITUATION: Being gripped and pushed against an object

If someone grips or holds your neck, shoulders, or lapels, and pushes you against an object such as a wall or a car, there are several techniques that you may be able to use, including the one shown here.

First, very quickly evaluate the situation. Make a mental note of where the person's balance is; this is to help you determine which technique to use.

Assess your attacker. Is he drunk? On drugs? Or the bully type?

If you are dealing with a bully, be aware that this type of person is usually showing off – "look at me, I'm so big and strong" – and looking for something to brag about.

If this is the case, it may be appropriate to make a lot of noise to help attract attention to your plight.

If the confrontation continues, and your attacker is standing with his left foot forward and most of his weight on the left leg, use the technique shown below.

TECHNIQUE

1. With the right hand grab his hair or ear.

2. Put the heel of your left hand onto his chin.

If your attacker has his right leg forward, you would need to alter your grip, so that the right hand grips his chin and the left hand grabs his ear or hair. Turn your body as one unit using the box step. and step off with the right foot.

If the man is drunk or on drugs this technique may not be enough on its own. It is a well known fact that such people seem to have phenomenal strength. If this is the case, a combination of techniques will be required.

3. With a very sharp, quick movement push with the left hand and pull with the right hand. At the same time turn your own body as one unit, step forward with your left foot, then move your right foot, using the box step on pp. 80–85.

4. By turning your body, you can direct the attacker's head directly into the object behind you.

Strike to neck

You will need power in your open hand to carry out this
technique successfully. As you start the open-hand movement,
grip his chin at the same time.

TECHNIQUE

1. Bring your right hand, palm up, towards his neck.

2. Strike the neck with the little finger edge of your hand.

3. Follow through with the strike and grab the hair or ear.

4. Grip the chin with the left hand. With a very sharp, quick movement, push with the left hand and pull with the right. At the same time, turn your body as one unit, using the box step on pp. 80–85. Step forward with the left foot and turn your body.

Uppercut

After gripping the ear with the left hand, the right can either strike the solar plexus or the chin. Or it can strike the solar plexus and then slide up to strike the chin.

TECHNIQUE

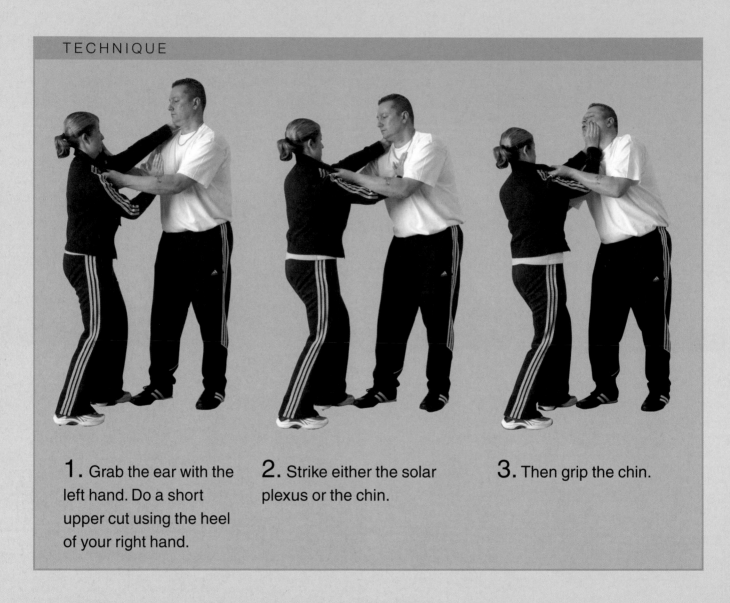

1. Grab the ear with the left hand. Do a short upper cut using the heel of your right hand.

2. Strike either the solar plexus or the chin.

3. Then grip the chin.

With a very sharp, quick movement, push with the right hand and pull with the left hand. At the same time, turn your body as one unit, using the box step.

Side kick

You can kick the shin with the side of your foot, stamp on the foot (even more effective in high heels), or strike with your knee into the groin, and then grip the chin and grab the ear. With a very sharp, quick movement push with the left hand and pull with the right. At the same time, turn your own body as one unit, using the box step.

With the kick/stamp technique remember to make sure that you always use the side of the foot and not the toes, as that can be quite painful to you.

TECHNIQUE

1. Continue by kicking the shin or knee.

2. Stamp on the foot. Or, from the kick to the shin, slide down the leg and then stamp on the foot.

3. Raise the knee and strike the groin.

Forward kick

Your attacker may anticipate that you will retaliate, so he may think he is being clever if he holds you with both hands, keeping his legs apart, and stretches forward to reach you.

TECHNIQUE

1. Keep the leg straight and kick between the attacker's legs.

2. Grab the ear and chin, then pull with the left hand and push with the right.

This situation is even better for you as all you have to do is keep your leg straight and swing it into an upward kick straight between his legs before proceeding to the pull and push technique.

With a very sharp and quick movement, push with the right hand and pull with the left hand. At the same time, turn your body as one unit, using the box step.

AWARENESS

- of his demeanour
- of where his balance or weight is
- of your surroundings
- of the overall situation
- of his condition (i.e. drunk, on drugs)

PSYCHOLOGY

- Consider what options are available to you.
- Once you have decided on the action to take, do it with strength and conviction.

AVOIDANCE

- Try to avoid anything that may make the situation worse.
- Avoid being submissive or giving that impression.

PHYSICAL

- Once you have evaluated all the facts and have decided what course of action to take, be strong in thought and determined in action.

SITUATION: Defence from the floor

In an ideal situation you would never be on the floor, but you may either fall, get tripped or be thrown onto the floor.

If you find yourself on the floor, with your attacker kneeling across your body, you must assess your attacker very quickly. Where is his weight or balance? And what is his state of mind?

If he is just pinning you to the floor by your shoulders or lapels, then you will probably have several seconds to evaluate the situation and think it through.

But if he has his hands on your throat, or his arm across your throat, and is cutting off your air supply, you will need to act very quickly, before you start to pass out.

The fear factor will be very strong in this situation, so don't forget to use it positively.

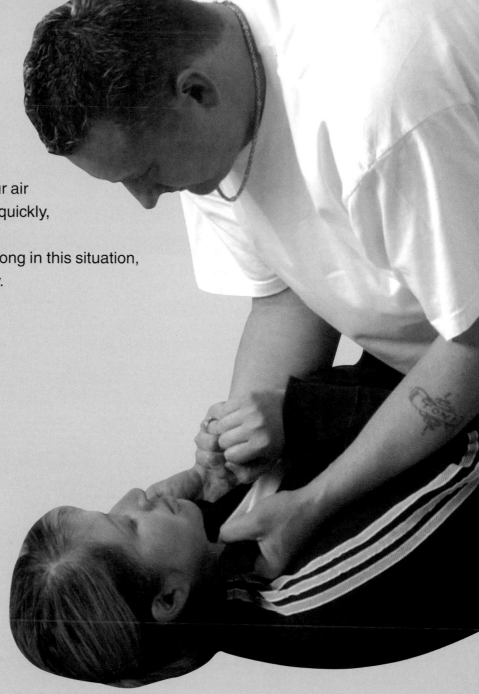

If you are being pinned to the floor
Evaluate your attacker's balance. If he is leaning forward and either strangling you or pinning you down by the shoulders or the lapels, his weight will be forward over the upper part of your body.

With this movement you will roll onto or towards your left side as you throw or push your attacker over your left shoulder. His head will probably come into contact with the floor, and this may stun him, or at least shock him into being unable to move for a few seconds, giving you the opportunity to get away.

TECHNIQUE

1. Gripping the chin with one hand and pulling the ear or hair with the other will be very effective, but you will need to add another movement to this technique.

2. As you pull on his right ear or hair with your left hand and grip his chin with your right hand, bring your right foot along the floor as close to your buttocks as you can.

If it does not, make sure you put as much distance as possible between you before he recovers from the shock of your retaliation.

Now consider what to do next. Can you call for help, or move away? Do not turn your back to your attacker.

3. With a very short, sharp movement, as you pull with your left hand and push with your right hand, push up with your right foot and leg, raising your hips towards your left side. If this movement is done very quickly, it should throw your attacker over your left shoulder or to the left side of your upper body.

If your arms are pinned to your sides

by the attacker either holding or kneeling on them, you can still get away from him.

1. Bring your knee up and strike him hard on the buttocks to move his body weight forward. You may have to strike hard and fast several times.

2. As you feel his weight going forwards, grab his shins and grip hard.

Remember, you must practise each of these movements on both sides. If you practise only on one side and someone attacks on the opposite side you can't say, "Sorry, but I can't work on this side"!

3. Place the foot of your raised knee firmly on the floor and push upwards, raising your hips. At the same time lift with your hands.

Turn the hips and shoulders and w the attacker over your ulder. Now quickly escape or distance between you.

AWARENESS

- of the position you are in
- of the place you are in
- of where your attacker's weight is
- of where your attacker's balance is
- Is he pinning you down or trying to strangle you?
- Is there anything or anyone close at hand that can be of help to you?

PSYCHOLOGY

- to be mentally alert
- determined not to be taken advantage of
- prepared to protect yourself with determination and intent
- prepared to change or adjust the technique as the situation changes

AVOIDANCE

- Avoid mentally telling yourself that you cannot do anything.
- Avoid any negative thoughts at all.
- Avoid being a victim.

PHYSICAL

- The majority of people think that if you are on the floor you will be unable to help yourself. But being on the floor can be a good position for defensive moves because you have both arms and legs available. Arms and legs are very useful tools, so use them with as much force and intent as you can muster.
- If you are on the floor and the attacker is standing, you can use your legs and feet for kicking out.
- If your attacker is by your head kicking you, your arms can be used to protect your head until there is an opportunity to grab his leg or foot, and twist it.

SITUATION: Aggressive handshake

Have you ever shaken someone's hand, only to find that they begin to squeeze very hard? This is nearly always done in front of other people, as the person doing the squeezing looks around very smugly, pleased that they have caught you out.

This type of person usually has a bully mentality, and is probably well known for his behaviour. You, unfortunately, have not heard anything about them until it is too late – usually after the incident.

As soon as you start to feel the pressure being applied to your hand, perform this counter technique very quickly.

Do not wait until he has squeezed your hand as tight as he can, as you will need to put a lot more power into the movement. It will also be more painful for you, although it should still work. However, you will need to be more determined and to use a lot more force.

This situation is very easy to deal with, providing you react very quickly.

1. Straighten the fingers and relax the hand being squeezed.

2. Put your left hand on his arm, with fingers together and the thumb close to his wrist.

3. Keep the squeezed hand relaxed with the fingers and thumb together.

4. With a very short, sharp movement, push down with the left hand and pull up with the right hand.

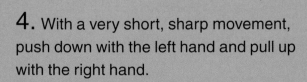

By this time it will be obvious why you have straightened your fingers and relaxed the hand. Relaxing the hand means that you can now fold it into a V shape or wedge, which will allow you to slide it out from your attacker's hand much more easily.

A word of warning – never place your left hand on his wrist with the thumb on one side and the palm/fingers on the other because if he is strong, or you mistime the pull and push technique, you may cause yourself quite a lot of damage and pain as your thumb is pushed back. So keep your fingers and thumb together.

wrong way

right way

The only drawback to this counter movement is that if you are wearing rings, the push and pull technique can cause some discomfort. Although having your hand squeezed with rings on can also be very painful.

Even though we do not shake hands on the other side (left hand) it is still a good idea to practise the movement on both sides.

This particular technique is the most basic of this group, but is still very effective. The other techniques have varying degrees of difficulty, with the last technique actually causing the attacker an arm injury.

SITUATION:
An man puts an unwanted arm about your waist

If you have ever experienced anything like this, you will know that it can be quite distressing or upsetting. If the attacker has a strong grip and is pulling you towards him, you feel that you do not have enough strength to push him away. In this situation you will have a small amount of time to consider what to do, but the first thing is to stay calm. Once you are calm and in control of your feelings, you can carry out the following technique.

1. Here, the man is on your right side, with his left arm around your waist.

2. Place your left hand firmly on his left hand to stop any further movement on his part.

3. Using the box step on pp. 80–85, step out with your right leg. This will leave a small gap between his left hand and your waist. Bend the fingers of your left hand to fill the gap. You will now be gripping his hand.

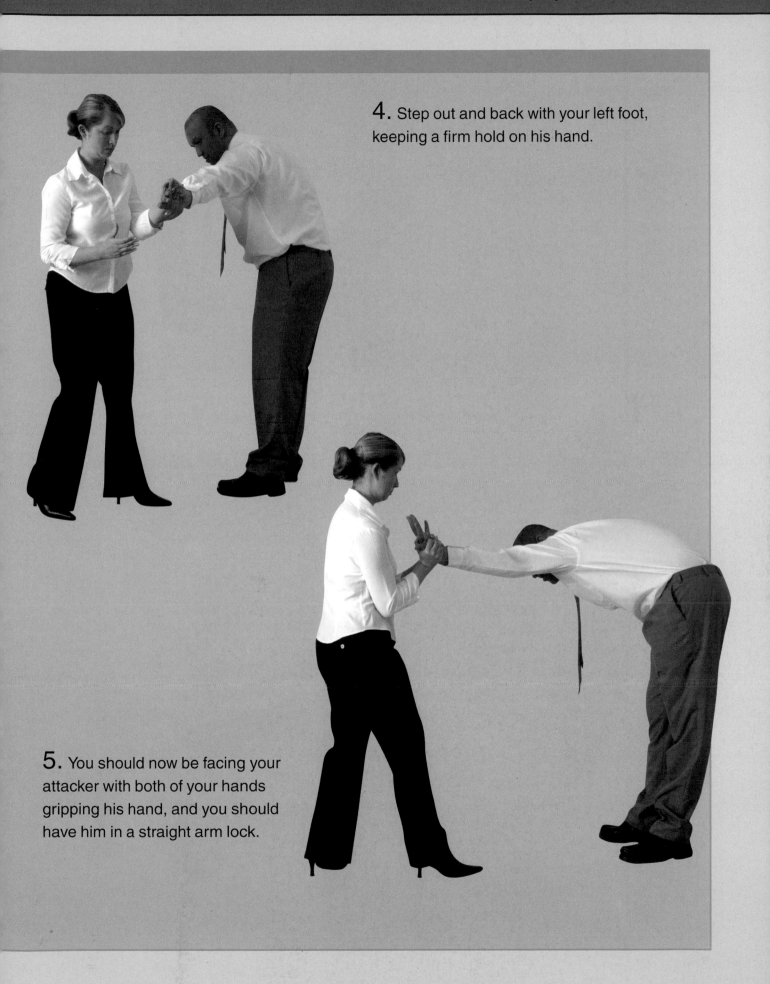

4. Step out and back with your left foot, keeping a firm hold on his hand.

5. You should now be facing your attacker with both of your hands gripping his hand, and you should have him in a straight arm lock.

Make sure that both your hands are on the back of his hand and that you are holding the hand firmly.

Although I have broken the movement down into four separate steps, when you perform the technique they should be almost as one.

To make the technique slightly more effective, once you have your attacker in a straight arm lock, take a pace back. This will make your attacker off balance.

If you really do not like this person, you can make sure that he does not try this again, if he has not already learnt his lesson.

Check which leg your weight is on, then bring the other leg up, keeping it straight, to kick your attacker in either the stomach or chest.

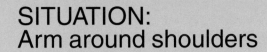

SITUATION:
Arm around shoulders

If the attacker puts his left arm around your shoulders you can use the same technique, but just adapt it slightly.

Here, the man is on your right side, with his left arm around your back and his hand on your left shoulder.

TECHNIQUE

1. Place your right hand firmly on his left hand.

2. Using the box step, step out with your right leg. This will leave a small gap between his left hand and your shoulder. Bend the fingers of your right hand to fill the gap. You will now be gripping his hand.

3. Place both the heels of your hands on the back of his hand. Make sure you are gripping the back of his hand.

4. Step out and back with your left foot. You should now be facing your attacker, with his arm in a straight arm/wrist lock.

5. Firmly push onto the back of his hand, knocking him off balance.

AWARENESS

- of where your own balance is (If you are off balance, you will not be able to proceed with this technique.)
- of where your attacker's balance is
- of your surroundings
- of any people about who are not his friends or associates

PSYCHOLOGY

- of what you can do
- of what your attacker is about to do or wants to do
- remaining calm but in control

AVOIDANCE

- As you start to feel the arm going around you, very quickly move away.
- As you feel the arm, make as much noise as possible, especially if you are in a populated area (i.e. "get off me" or "don't touch me").

PHYSICAL

- Although you do not have to be very strong to make these techniques work, you will have to be forceful in your movements.
- If, when you have put the arm/wrist lock on, your attacker bends his elbow, just continue with the push by stepping forward. You may need to step forward a few times, but continue to push hard. Then get yourself away from him.

SITUATION: In a lift

Ideally you would never have to use a lift, but sometimes this is not a viable option (i.e.a high-rise building or a tower block). If you find yourself alone in a lift with an unsavoury character, it may be a problem, as you have nowhere to escape to until the lift reaches the next floor. So, for several seconds, you will be completely on your own.

With this situation psychology will really come into its own, as you will need all your mental ability to deal with it. Again, do not panic or start acting nervously, because this will be a signal of your vulnerability and will immediately give him confidence. Signs of nervousness include chewing your lips, continually touching your face, fiddling with your fingers or rings and nervously looking around with your eyes lowered.

Remain upright and confident. If you are shaking in your shoes, don't show it. Remember that your body language (i.e. posture) will be communicating a great deal about you.

Place yourself next to the controls so that, if the need arises, you will be able to activate the alarm. But keep in mind that although you may have activated the alarm, the lift will continue to the next designated floor.

If possible, place yourself with your back to the side of the lift next to the controls.

If you are carrying a bag

If you are carrying a bag, briefcase or umbrella, hold it in front of you, so that it is between you and the man. This will give you the psychological advantage of having a barrier between you.

TECHNIQUE

1. Place the bag between you.

2. If he comes towards you, raise the bag.

As soon as possible get out of the lift, and get help.

3. Push the bag into him very strongly.

If he lunges at you so quickly that you are unable to bring the bag up, just push it forwards as hard as possible, either using your hand on the bag or your thigh. Now bring the bag up.

If you have no bag

If you find yourself with nothing to help you, or if your attacker has got past your bag and actually grabs hold of you by the shoulders, lapels or neck, use the technique below (see also pp. 122–131).

TECHNIQUE

2. Put the heel of your right hand onto your attacker's chin or grip the chin, and with your left hand grab his hair or ear.

1. Here, your attacker is standing with right foot forward and most of his weight on his right leg.

3. With a very sharp, quick movement push with the right hand and pull with the left hand. At the same time, turn your body as one unit, stepping out with the right foot and turning so that you are facing left. Use the box step on pp. 80–85.

By turning your body, you can direct the attacker's head directly into the wall of the lift. Depending on your position in the lift, direct his head into the wall closest to you, whether it is behind you or beside you.

Then get out of the lift as soon as possible and get help.

If your attacker has his left leg forward, you will need to alter your movements so the left hand grips his chin and the right hand grabs his ear or hair. Step out with the left foot and turn so you are facing right, using the box step.

AWARENESS

- of the unsavoury character's body language
- of the unsavoury character's position in the lift
- of your own body language
- of your position in the lift
- of what you have with you that can offer protection

PSYCHOLOGY

Your own
- mentally and physically alert
- prepared for what may happen
- upright and confident

The unsavoury character
- If he has robbery in mind his body language and mental attitude will be conveying this, which may make you feel uncomfortable.
- If he has rape in mind, his body language will be very different and will definitely be conveying his thoughts. This may make you feel ill at ease, or even fearful.

AVOIDANCE

- Leave the lift with other people.
- Leave the lift at the earliest opportunity.
- Avoid looking down or giving any indication of being submissive.

PHYSICAL

- Be prepared to fight and fight hard for your protection.
- As in all close-quarter fighting, you can carry out any of the following actions:
  you can pinch (very painful if it is on the upper part of and inside the thigh)
  bite (whatever is closest to you)
  scratch (any exposed skin)
  push or strike with your open hand very hard on your attacker's nose
  if you have long finger nails you can scratch down his face.

SITUATION: Walking the dog

This situation is slightly different from any of the others. Because the majority of dogs are just family pets, they have not been trained to defend you, so you cannot rely on the dog to protect you. They may, however, respond to your distress by jumping up or barking.

Also, when walking the dog, you usually carry very little with you that you could use to defend yourself. However, think about what you do have.

If you are carrying a lead, it can be used in defence. You may possibly have a set of keys, which can also be used to protect yourself.

If the lead is expandable, the plastic handle is usually quite strong and can be used as:

- a guard, to either stop the strike, or protect yourself against a strike.
- to deflect or ward off a punch, open-hand strike or strike with a weapon.
- or to retaliate with a sideways strike or a straight hit to your attacker's face or body

Defending with a strike

To block a punch from your attacker bring the lead up, then
strike forward into the attacker's face.

TECHNIQUE

1. Your attacker lunges towards you.

2. Block him with the lead.

3. Strike towards his face.

Defending with a front strike

Block a left-handed punch with your right arm. At the same
time, strike forward with the lead into your attacker's face.

TECHNIQUE

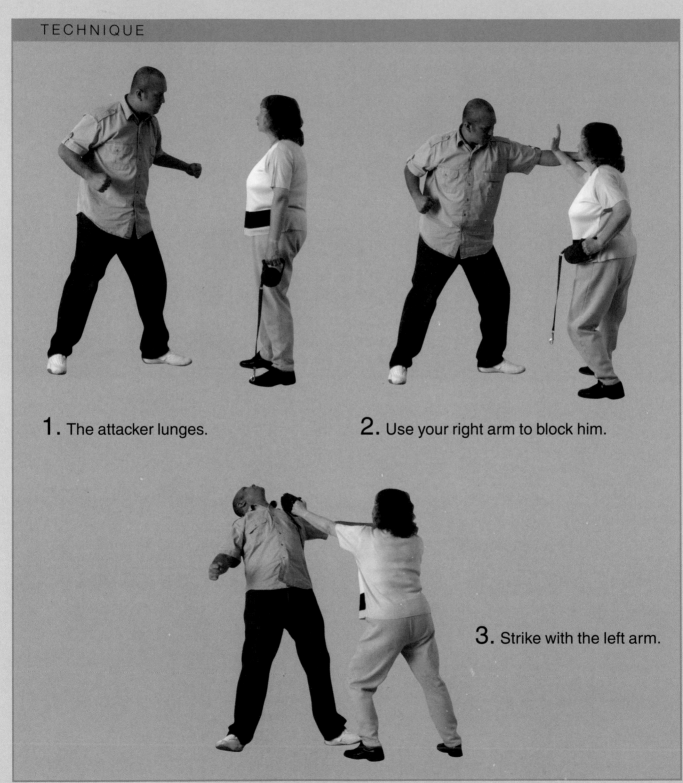

1. The attacker lunges.

2. Use your right arm to block him.

3. Strike with the left arm.

Defending with a thin lead

If the lead is just a leather or material strap with a metal hook at the end, it can also be used quite effectively.

Keep the open, looped end over your wrist, and hold the strap. With the other hand swing the lead in a circle. If you keep this between yourself and the attacker it may keep him at bay, while you back up.

If he still comes towards you, flick out the lead with the metal part going towards your attacker. This should make him flinch back and be wary of you, giving you time to get away, get help or gain sufficient time to re-evaluate the situation.

TECHNIQUE

1. Swing the lead in a circular movement.

2. Flick the metal hook of the lead towards your attacker's head or face.

3. With a sideways movement, swing the metal hook into the side of your attacker's head.

AWARENESS

- of your surroundings – parkland or woodland, hillside, populated area, near lake
- of other people who may be around
- of what you are carrying
- of any public buildings nearby, if you are in a built-up area

PSYCHOLOGY

- to be alert to what is around you
- prepared to adjust your mental preparations to your surroundings as they change

AVOIDANCE

- If possible, do not go out alone. If you know someone in your immediate vicinity who is a dog owner, try to arrange to go walking with them.
- Avoid any indication of fear or panic.

PHYSICAL

- Use whatever is available to you – either what you are carrying or what is around you (sticks, stones, lumps of wood, rubbish) – for defensive movements or for throwing.

Defending with keys

Your keys make a useful defence weapon at close quarters. Hold them in the palm of your hand – use your strongest hand – with either one or two of the tips protruding through your fingers.

You can now use the fist/keys to strike your attacker, or slash across his face.

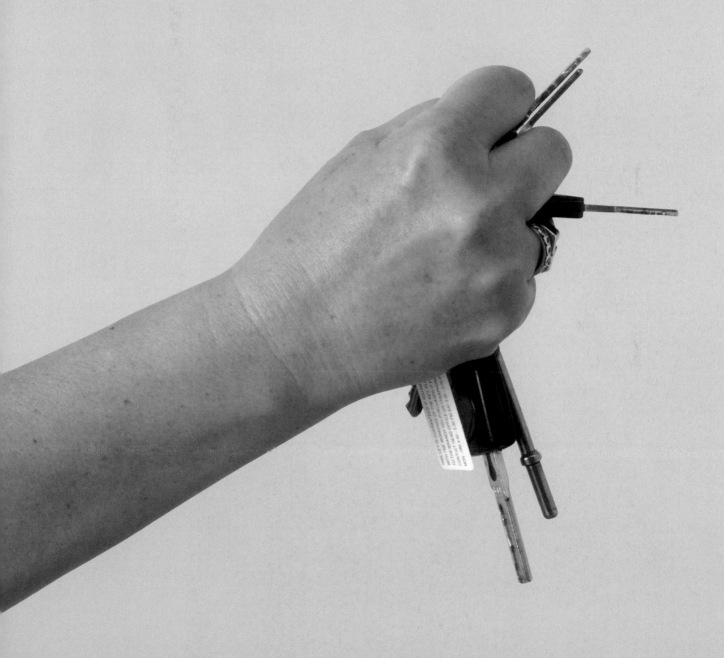

TECHNIQUE

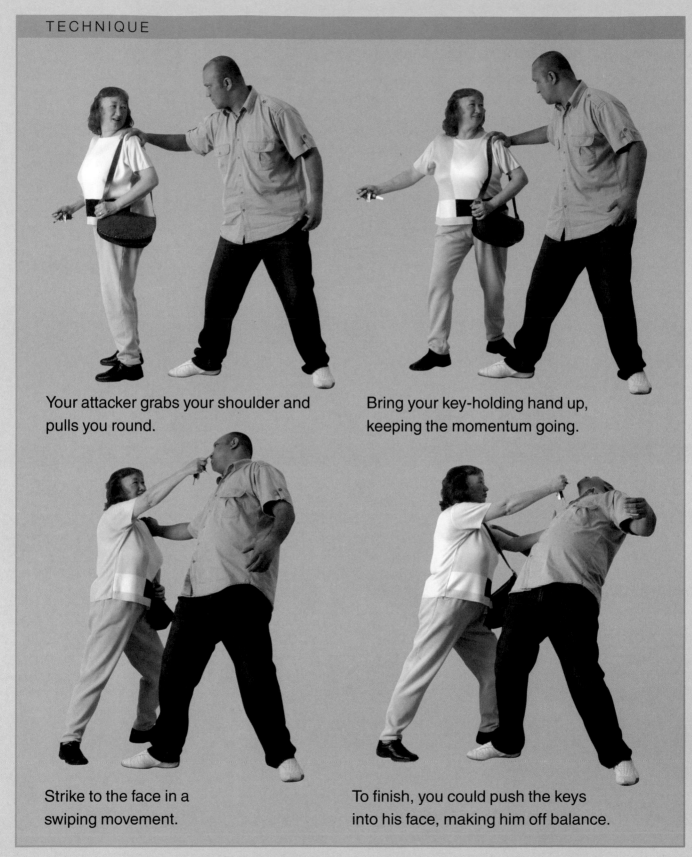

Your attacker grabs your shoulder and pulls you round.

Bring your key-holding hand up, keeping the momentum going.

Strike to the face in a swiping movement.

To finish, you could push the keys into his face, making him off balance.

The shock effect should give you valuable seconds in which to get away, and get help.

SITUATION: In a car park

A number of car parks now have surveillance cameras, so if you are lucky enough to have such a car park in your area, use it, even if it is a little more expensive than one without cameras.

If at all possible park close to a light/bright area and close to an exit. Try to keep to a busy area.

If the car park does not have surveillance cameras, when you return to your car keep the following points in mind:

On approaching your car, if you think there is one too many shadows close to the car, walk past it, looking all around to see if you can actually spot anyone.

If your senses, or awareness, are making you feel uneasy, leave the area immediately and get help.

Do not forget to look under the car, just in case, although this is not necessary if your car is very low to the ground.

If it looks like someone is near your car:

- go back into the shopping centre or high street and get help
- if you have a mobile, phone the police
- if the car park has attendants then get help from them

Do not go back to your car until you have help with you.

Attacked at the side of your car

If you are attacked by your car, and the assailant grabs your throat, coat, lapels or shoulders from the front, and pushes you onto the car, carry out the following technique.

If your attacker is standing with right foot forward and most of his weight on his right leg, put the heel of your right hand onto his chin, or grip the chin, and with your left hand grab his hair or ear.

With a very sharp and quick movement, push with the right hand and pull with the left hand. At the same time, turn your own body as one unit, stepping out with the right foot and turning so you are facing left as you use the box step on pp 80–85.

TECHNIQUE

1. An attacker grabs both your shoulders and pushes you back onto the car.

2. Grab his chin, hair or ear, and carry out the pull and push movement as described above.

3. Push with your right hand and pull with the left hand, directing his head into the car.

As soon as you can, get away and get help.

Attacker pushes you

If your attacker has pushed you so that you are facing the car, and then continues to push you against the car, the chances are that he will have one hand pushing you in the middle of your back, so that his other hand is free to search your pockets, rifle your bag or do whatever he has in mind.

If he has his left hand pressing into your back, you must push against the car slightly to give yourself a small amount of space. Then step back slightly with your left foot and step across your

TECHNIQUE

1. Your attacker has pushed you against your car.

2. Give yourself a little space to manoeuvre.

front with the right leg. Turn your body to the left and, at the same time, use the fist movement on pp. 86–90 to deflect the hand pushing into your back.

If you are carrying a bag or umbrella, either of them can be used as a lever or to strike your attacker. Then get yourself away and get help.

Keep in mind that goods, whether cheap, expensive, money or mobile, can be replaced, your life cannot.

3. Step across your front with the right leg. At the same time, turn your body and bring up your left arm in a block.

4. Step forwards. With your right hand either punch or push your attacker.

AWARENESS

- of your position in the car park
- of who is around and their body language
- when you are leaving or returning to your car
- of other people who may be of use to you
- when you are putting shopping in your boot

PSYCHOLOGY

- Do not get caught out by being unprepared.
- Always keep in mind your personal safety.

AVOIDANCE

- If you have the choice of a multi-storey or single-floor car park, choose the single or else the ground floor.
- Although we all have to go to shopping centres etc, always keep the safety aspect in mind.
- Keep clear of any dark or isolated areas.

PHYSICAL

- Keep in mind how you can deal with any possible attacker in the area that you are in.
- If necessary, change your plans as the situation changes.

SITUATION: Grabbed from behind

If your attacker should come at you from behind, the most effective technique is the box step on pp. 80–85 and the fist technique, using either one fist or both fists, on pp. 86–90.

Shoulder grab

With this movement, it does not matter whether he has grabbed you with his left or right hand, although the end result will be different.

If he grabs your right shoulder, using the box step method, circle the right foot around. At the same time, bring your left fist up to break his grip. You should now be facing your attacker.

Now choose a technique that will suit you and the situation best. You could use a counter strike with one or both fists, an open hand or a lead or make as much noise as you can. The course of action you choose will depend on your surroundings (i.e. whether you are in a populated area or not).

TECHNIQUE – GRABBED WITH LEFT HAND

1. You are grabbed with the left hand from behind.

2. Step round and back, bringing the right arm up to block.

3. Step forward with the left leg and strike your attacker's face with your left hand.

TECHNIQUE – GRABBED WITH RIGHT HAND

1. You are grabbed with the right hand from behind.

2. Swing round and back, knocking his arm away with your right hand.

3. Step forward with your left foot and firmly push him in the back with your left hand.

Bear hug

An attacker may grab you from behind in a bear hug. The technique below explains how to escape.

1. The attacker enfolds you in a bear hug.

2. Clasp your hands together and bring them up sharply as you drop down.

3. Twist your body, and elbow him strongly in the chest.

4. Now use your right hand to push his head back.

SITUATION: Being gripped from behind

You may find yourself in a situation where your attacker has gripped both of your wrists and is holding them behind your back. He may be doing this to prevent you from moving in order to allow another attacker to do whatever it is they have in mind for you.

This situation will be very frightening and will require a lot more determination and effort from you. Do your best to remain calm and act quickly.

The attacker in front of you will need to be dealt with very quickly before he does anything to you and before you can deal with the attacker who is gripping your wrists.

The most effective technique is to make sure that all your weight is on your left leg before using your right leg in a forward kick to the groin of the front attacker. Make sure that he is in range and keep your leg straight. Before the first attacker has time to recover, continue swiftly with the following technique.

Once you have kicked the first attacker in the groin with your right leg, place the right foot back on the ground. At the same time turn your body sharply to to the left, which should break your attacker's hold on your left wrist. Place the back of your right hand against your back. Hold it there very tightly (imagine that your arm is locked to your back).

Grip your attacker's right wrist with your left hand. Then, with a short, sharp movement (using your body), break your attacker's grip on your right hand.

Sometimes with this movement, because it is done very sharply and quickly, the attacker may actually lose his balance. If this should happen, release your grip quickly so he does not pull you down onto the ground as well.

If he does not lose his balance and is still gripping you, step out with the right leg (using the box step on pp. 80–85) so that you end up facing your attacker. Your left hand should still be gripping his right wrist.

As you turn you should have your attacker's right hand so that the back is facing you. Place the heels of both your hands on the back of his right hand. Push with your right hand and pull with your left hand, so that you twisting his hand anticlockwise. As you twist, your attacker's hand/wrist, step back and round with your left leg. This will put him into the path of the first attacker. Make sure that both of your hands are placed onto the back of his hand and that you are twisting his hand firmly.

TECHNIQUE

1. One attacker holds your wrists while another comes towards you.

2. Put your weight on your left foot. Raise and straighten your right leg.

3. Kick your attacker in the groin.

4. Turn your body sharply to the left and press the back of your right hand firmly against your back. Grip his right wrist with your left hand.

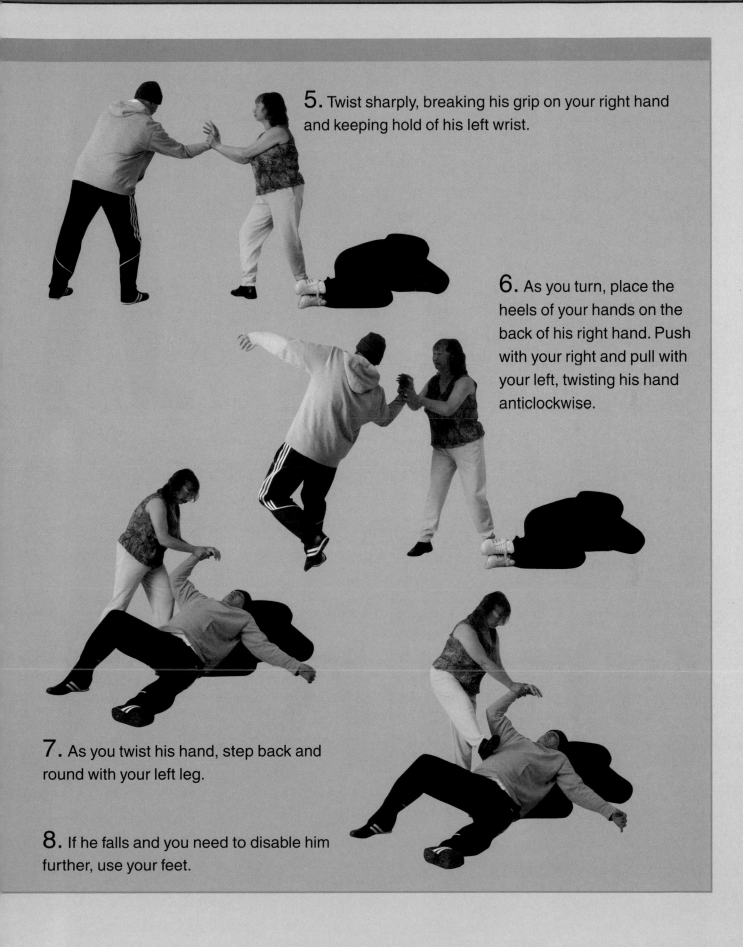

5. Twist sharply, breaking his grip on your right hand and keeping hold of his left wrist.

6. As you turn, place the heels of your hands on the back of his right hand. Push with your right and pull with your left, twisting his hand anticlockwise.

7. As you twist his hand, step back and round with your left leg.

8. If he falls and you need to disable him further, use your feet.

SITUATION:
An attacker punches to your face

This technique can be used whether your attacker has a knife, a bar or just his fist.

If your attacker is punching towards your face with his right arm/fist, use the following technique.

Using the box step, step your left foot to C3 and your right to C1. This should be one step rather than two. At the same time, bring both your fists up. This movement should bring you to the outside of your attacker's arm.

Bringing your fists up should protect your face and upper body if he should try to redirect his arm by swinging it back towards you.

Move your left arm forward and under your

TECHNIQUE

1. Box step LF to C3 and RF to C1. Bring your fists up.

2. Move your left arm forward and under his arm, so the hand is by his elbow.

3. Place your right hand on his forearm or wrist.

attacker's arm. Ensure that your left hand comes to the inside of your attacker's elbow.

With a sharp and powerful pull and push movement, pull back towards you with your left hand and push very sharply with your right hand. This should push your attacker's own fist into his face or neck, depending on the angle.

Sometimes with this movement, if it is done very quickly, your attacker may be taken by surprise, overbalancing and falling back. If this should happen, release your grip and allow him to fall, so that he does not drag you down with him.

Then quickly get yourself away and get help.

4. Pull towards you with your left hand and push sharply with your right hand.

5. If your attacker falls, release him quickly.

chapter 8 **sexual interference**

Most women dread a sexual attack. However, with the right frame of mind, and having practised your techniques, you may be able to keep yourself safe.

The attacks in this section are probably the most distressing, because the majority are carried out by someone we know, either as a work colleague, a friend or a family member.

So that person will probably have a very good knowledge of your day to day routine as well as your strengths and weaknesses. They may also know that you are reading or learning from this book or another self-protection book.

You will be faced with the problem of how to deal with the attack and whether you should report it. There is a strong psychology element to attacks in this section, as your attacker will be relying on your mental anguish and confusion, and hoping that you could not bear to upset the people in your personal circle by accusing him.

As he will never openly admit to his attack, it will be your word against his. This can very difficult and stressful for all concerned, putting a lot of pressure on other members of the family or on friends, who will have to decide who to believe. Invariably this causes problems for them and may cause a split within your personal circle. This, in turn, will put even more pressure on you.

After the attack he will more than likely show deep remorse, apologising and promising that it will not happen again. But if he gets away with it this time, he knows that he can get away with it again.

The emotions that you will feel once the attack starts will probably go from, "He can't be doing this" to feeling "What have I done to encourage this?" to feeling degraded.

First you must overcome these feelings and any thoughts that you have somehow bought this attack upon yourself. This attack is not your fault. You have probably done nothing to encourage it.

If he has pinned you down on the floor or a bed, evaluate his balance. If he is leaning forwards and pinning you down by the shoulder or the upper part of your body, his weight will be forward over the upper part of your body. He will probably be using just one hand or arm for this, so that his other hand is free to act in some way.

SITUATION:
If he is using his right hand/arm to pin you down

Gripping his chin with one hand and pulling his ear/hair with the other will be very effective. If you are pulling on his left ear/hair with your left hand and your right hand is gripping his chin, bring your left foot along the floor as close to your buttocks as possible.

    With a very short and sharp but strong movement, as you pull with your right hand and push with your left hand, push up with your left foot, raising your hips towards your right side. If done

quickly enough, this movement will throw him over your right shoulder or right upper body.

If you have not been able to get yourself clear of him sufficiently to get away, you can counter strike with your fist or open hand. Or, if the movement has made your body turn, you may be in a position to either kick or stamp down with the heel of your foot.

Now get yourself away from the situation as quickly as possible.

1. Grip his chin with the right hand and grab his ear/hair with the left. Bring the right leg up, placing the foot firmly on the floor.

2. Push up with the right leg and raise your hips. At the same time, pull with your left hand and push with your right.

3. Push him over your shoulder, then make your escape.

AWARENESS

- With most situations your awareness may be heightened by your surroundings, but in this type of situation you will not normally be 'on guard'. As you are within your own personal circle, you will normally be quite relaxed. Although you may become aware that something has changed, you may not be sure what, which in itself can be disturbing.

PSYCHOLOGY

- There will be a very strong psychological problem going on once an attack has started, but you must be positive and very determined not to allow it to continue. You must repel any unwanted advances from any member of your family and show them that you are not a willing victim.

AVOIDANCE

- Avoid being flirty or showing any overly friendly attention to any one individual.
- Avoid being alone with any one individual on too many occasions.
- Avoid any situation that may encourage unwanted attention.

PHYSICAL

- If you are touched anywhere that feels different (i.e. more intimate) repulse that touch with determination. Also make sure that the attacker knows that this type of touch, behaviour or action is not acceptable to you. If the attacker will not accept a verbal rebuff, you may need to reinforce it with a slap to the face or something similar.

Physical abuse

As with rape, physical abuse is among the very high percentage of assaults committed by partners, ex-partners, husbands or ex-husbands.

It has long been a belief that what happens behind closed doors within the family environment has nothing to do with anyone else, which allows the abuser to mentally, physically or sexually abuse his wife or his children.

The unfortunate part of this is that all children learn how to behave, how to interact with other people and how to treat other people by observing their parents. So, if a child has an abusive parent or parents, they may grow up not knowing any other form of behaviour. They will associate 'friendship' with bad or unacceptable behaviour and 'love' with beatings and foul language, thus perpetuating the abusive cycle.

The media – radio, television and newspapers – regularly report women or children being abused, but this is seldom until the abuse has ended in the death of the victim.

Providing the police have sufficient evidence they can then proceed against the abuser, which will hopefully keep the other members of the family safe. This particular shift in attitude is very welcome, and in time should reduce the number of abusive incidents and deaths. But the police need to know about the assaults before they can do anything about them.

If you are in fear of any form of abuse to yourself or another member of your family, you must seek help. The first step, which is probably the biggest and most difficult, is realising that you do need help. The second step, which can be equally difficult, is to get help on where to go and who to speak to.

If you are still at school, try to talk to someone there whom you feel comfortable with and who will listen. If there is no one there whom you feel you can approach, try a friendly or caring relative outside your immediate family circle. If there is no one you feel that you can trust (and it does not matter how young or old you are), contact one of the numerous helplines. If they cannot help you directly, they can at least put you in touch with some one who can.

In all cases of abuse, you will invariably feel alone and isolated. You will probably have been threatened, particularly if you should try to tell anyone. If you have facial injuries you are made to lie about them. If the injuries are such that you have to go to, or end up in, hospital, tell one of the nurses or the doctor (if you have been left alone with them and are able to talk to them).

But you must tell someone who can help, and sooner rather than later.

Being attacked by someone with a weapon can be very frightening, but there are some basic techniques you can use to defend yourself.

A knife attack can be very frightening, especially if you have never trained to use or understand this type of weapon.

The most fearful thing about a knife attack is the thought of being cut, stabbed, slashed or even killed. As a result the victim often freezes and is unable to do anything in the way of self-protection.

Before any techniques can be used effectively, you must control your fear of the knife. You must accept the fact that you may get hurt, possibly fatally. If you find that the possibility of being hurt is increasing by the minute, it is better to deliberately take a wound to a non-essential area. Although I hope that you will never be faced with having to make a decision like that.

Once you accept the fact that you may get hurt, the fear of the knife will lessen and you will be in a better position to take control of the situation, or be able to use self-protection techniques. No matter how wonderful or effective the technique, if you are afraid of the knife, it simply will not work for you at that particular moment.

Ask yourself how many times you have used a knife in a kitchen to cut up vegetables, meat and so on. Are you afraid of those knives? The chances are that you have cut yourself with a kitchen knife several times, but you are not afraid of using them again.

If you should happen to have a knife on you when you are attacked, be aware that unless you are very skilful, the knife could be taken from you and used against you. So, even if your attacker was not armed initially, he may well be by the end.

In this country it is illegal to carry a knife. But if you are attacked in your home, you might find yourself with a kitchen knife or some other type of knife.

The only difference between the kitchen knife and the attacker's knife is the intent.

Using the knife hilt

If you find yourself in a situation where you wish to use a knife for self-protection, you should hold it in a non-threatening way. This means keeping the knife out of obvious view.

If you are attacked with a club, stick, knife or fist, you can then use the knife to block or deflect the attack.

After you have deflected or blocked an attack you can then use the knife to counter attack. With the counter attack you could use the hilt of the knife to strike your attacker.

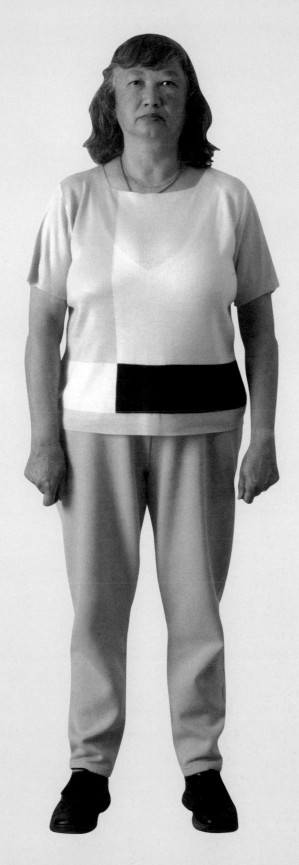 

Holding a knife in a non-threatening way – front view.   Holding a knife in non-threatening way – side view.

1. Your attacker threatens you with a slashing movement of his knife.

2. Using the box step, step with the right foot and, at the same time, bring the right arm up to block the knife.

3. Push slightly with the left hand to move his knife away from you. Strike his face or neck with the hilt of your knife.

TECHNIQUE

1. Your attacker makes a stabbing movement towards you.

2. Using the box step, step with the left leg. At the same time, bring both arms up to block the knife. Then push slightly on his stabbing arm.

3. Push your weight forward onto your left leg. At the same time, strike your attacker's head with the hilt of your knife.

TECHNIQUE

1. Your attacker stabs downward towards you.

2. Using the box step, step with the left leg. At the same time, bring both arms up to block the knife. Push on your attacker's arm to move the knife away from you.

3. Depending on the angle of the attacker, strike at his kidneys or ribs with the hilt of your knife.

SITUATION: Knife attack

In most situations, the way your attacker holds the knife will give you some indication as to how he plans to use it. The two most common ways of holding a knife are shown below.

In the case of a knife attack, and if you are unarmed, you will inevitably need to perform more than one technique.

If the attacker holds the knife like this, it probably means that he is planning to strike downwards or to the side.

If he holds the knife like this, he can strike by thrusting forward or swing the knife from side to side in a threatening manner.

Blocking using a bag

A bag or briefcase can be very effective for defence against a knife. If the attacker makes a slashing movement, you can use the bag to take the force of the knife and protect yourself. Use the bag to push against your attacker

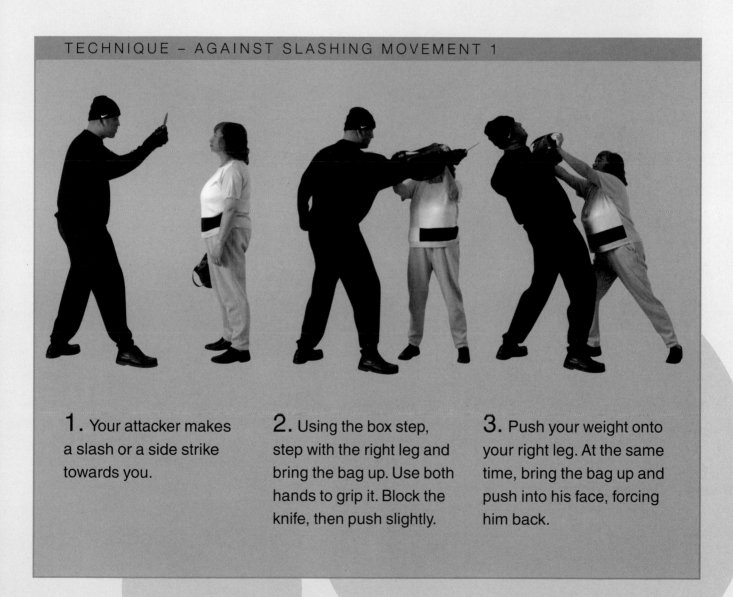

TECHNIQUE – AGAINST SLASHING MOVEMENT 1

1. Your attacker makes a slash or a side strike towards you.

2. Using the box step, step with the right leg and bring the bag up. Use both hands to grip it. Block the knife, then push slightly.

3. Push your weight onto your right leg. At the same time, bring the bag up and push into his face, forcing him back.

TECHNIQUE – AGAINST SLASHING MOVEMENT 2

1. Your attacker makes a side strike or a slashing movement.

2. Step back with the left leg and grip the bag with both hands.

3. As soon as the attacker's hand has passed you, bring the bag up.

4. Step forward with the left leg and push your bag into his face or upper body. Push hard to make him lose his balance.

Blocking using an umbrella

If you do not have a bag, but you do have a rolled-up newspaper or an umbrella, use the following technique.

TECHNIQUE – AGAINST STABBING MOVEMENT

1. Your attacker stabs straight towards you with the knife.

2. Using the box step, step with the left leg. At the same time, bring the umbrella up with one hand and use the other to do a double block. Push slightly on the attacker's arm.

From a stabbing movement use the box step, so that you are level with the attacker's arm (preferably on the outside of the arm). Use the umbrella to strike down VERY HARD onto the attacker's arm, and then strike his upper body – neck, throat, face – whatever is easiest to reach.

3. Grip the umbrella with both hands and strike down very hard on the attacker's arm.

4. Redirect the umbrella towards your attacker's head, striking him as hard as you possibly can.

If your attacker uses a slashing movement, you will need to jump back slightly, again using the umbrella to strike the arm that is holding the knife.

Depending on the angle of his arm you may also be able to strike his upper body, face, and neck. If the arm is too high, strike to the groin or stomach with the point of the umbrella. If you also have a bag push it into your attacker's face.

If you are unable to move back because of a wall or some other obstacle, you may be able to move sideways. Always move in the same direction as the knife. If the knife movement is right to left, then move to the left.

TECHNIQUE – AGAINST SLASHING MOVEMENT

1. Your attacker makes a side swipe or a slashing movement.

2. Step or jump back so that you are out of reach. Hold the umbrella with both hands.

This way, by the time the knife reaches you, there will be less force behind the strike, and you can more easily proceed to retaliate.

Unless you are very skilled, never attempt to grab the knife arm. If you find you are too close to strike comfortably, use your bag, umbrella or any other article or device that you have with you and push it straight into the attacker's face.

Remember, the attacker has a plan and is only looking for an opportunity. The attacker will assume that you will just freeze with fear, so if you retaliate the shock usually keeps the attacker off-guard, enabling you to take control of the situation.

3. Once the knife hand has passed you, step forward with your left leg, moving your weight onto it. At the same time, bring the umbrella up and strike under his arm.

4. Keep the upward movement strong and push up and forward, forcing him back and yourself away.

If you have nothing with you

that would help with your protection, then the following technique may be helpful.

Using the box step, step out the left foot to C3 and the right foot to C1. This should be one step rather than two. At the same time bring both of your fists up. This movement should bring you to the outside of your attacker's arm.

As soon as you are able to, make your escape and get help.

TECHNIQUE

1. Your attacker uses a straight thrust with the knife in his right hand.

2. Use the box step so that you are outside his arm. Bring both fists up to protect your face and upper body if he tries to redirect his arm.

3. Move your left arm forward, under and inside your attacker's arm. Ensure that your left hand is on the inside of your attacker's elbow.

4. Place your right hand on to your attacker's forearm, close to his wrist. With a sharp and powerful pull and push movement, pull back towards you with your left hand and push very sharply with your right hand.

5. This should push your attacker's fist or knife towards his face or neck, depending on the angle. If done powerfully, the movement could make your attacker fall. Make sure he does not drag you down as well. Get yourself away quickly.

AWARENESS

- of your attacker's state of mind
- of your attacker's body language
- of your own body language
- of your surroundings and whether they can be of help to you or not

PSYCHOLOGY

- Remain calm and confident. Try to breathe deeply and slowly. This will focus your mind on your breathing rather than the situation, thus helping you to remain calm.
- Retain a state of alertness.
- At all times be prepared to be hurt (this will take away the fear of being hurt).

AVOIDANCE

- Avoid showing any fear or distress.
- Avoid say something along the lines of "please don't hurt me". If you have to say anything at all then say "no no no NO NO" very loudly and forcefully.

PHYSICAL

- With defence movements against a knife attack everything you do must be done with force and determination; it is no good at all to be limp wristed about it.

chapter 10 at home

When you are at home, you feel safe and relaxed. The last thing on your mind is self-defence until you are faced with an unexpected situation that puts you in danger.

If you are at home alone, what do you do to ensure that no one can wander in?

Do you do any of the following?

- leave front and back doors unlocked
- leave windows either open or unlocked
- lock just the front door
- lock both doors at all times

If you leave a door unlocked or open, perhaps because your friend will be arriving shortly, you may find that the person who has just walked in is not the person you are expecting.

This can lead to a number of complications, depending on the situation you now find yourself in.

Keep your home secure.

RAPE

If the intruder has rape on his mind, he may interpret the fact that the door was open as an invitation to come in, implying that you will go along with anything he has in mind.

The rapist will invariably have a plan of action. He will just be looking for an opportunity. In some cases, he has already picked his victim, and knows exactly what he is going to do and how to do it.

This makes the crime premeditated and much more difficult for you to deal with, as the rapist will have considered all eventualities and will have already prepared for them.

Never say to a rapist, "please don't do this" or words to that effect. The only word he will hear, or choose to hear, is the word "please", and again he may take it as an indication that you are a willing partner. Many court cases fail because the rapist took the wording of his victim as agreement to the act.

If you are able to talk to him, then do so in a calm and authoritative way. Many a situation has been stopped because the victim was able to talk her way out of it. If the situation requires you to shout, keep the wording short and sharp – "No, No, No!"

Always stay calm, and try to give yourself time by talking. This will enable you to take control of the situation and allow you to think out what to do in a defensive action.

Continually evaluate the situation. As it changes, you must keep assessing and evaluating what is happening, so that you can keep yourself as safe as possible.

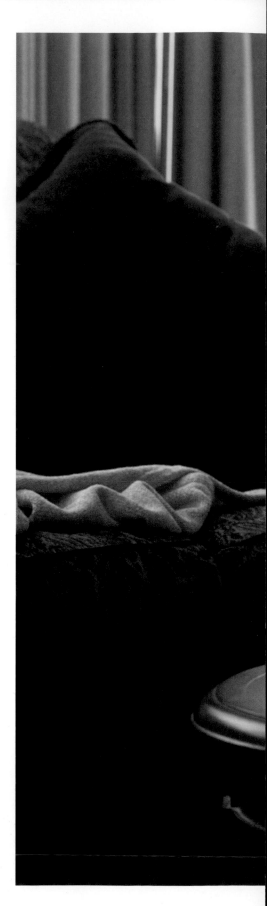

Your home should be your refuge.

ROBBERY

Most robberies are committed by the opportunist, who sees an easy target, then goes in as fast as he can, grabbing whatever he can see and making his escape very quickly. To make sure that there is little opportunity for anyone to catch him on your premises, he will try not to be seen or heard by anyone and usually makes very little noise. Despite this, he may leave your house or room in a complete mess.

If the robbery is premeditated, the robber will have already picked his victim or property and planned for all eventualities. He also knows what it is he wants to steal and will make straight for that item or items, then make good his escape.

If the intruder only has robbery on his mind but finds you in his way, you must try to evaluate him. What state of mind is he in? Is he armed with a knife, gun, or any other form of weapon? All of this must be done in a matter of seconds.

Do you have anything within reach to protect yourself? Can you get out of the house, fast?

If you are able to get out of the house without having to go past the intruder, do so – and quickly. But at no time should you turn your back on him, unless he has not seen you. Go immediately to a neighbour's house and call the police.

If you are trapped, and the intruder considers you a threat then you must deal with that situation. Do not panic. If you are able to get to a room and lock the door then do so. If you do not have a lock on the door but you do have a rubber wedge, then put that under the door. This will make it far more difficult for the intruder to get into the room. If you have a telephone in the room then call for help, or if possible get out through the window, or even shout for help.

If he is armed with a gun, then bide your time and do not try anything that might result in you, or members of your family, getting shot.

At all times you must consider the position you are in – not only your own safety but that of your family or friends.

AWARENESS

- When you are at home you are generally relaxed and not thinking or reacting with awareness. But, having said this, you may suddenly feel uncomfortable, but be unable to decide what has caused the feeling. If you should start to feel that something is not right, proceed around your home with extreme caution. If you can hear any noises that you know should not be there, get out of the house as quickly as you can.

PSYCHOLOGY

- At this point, your nervous and sensory awareness will be heightened. You must think very carefully but quickly about what action needs to be taken, or should be taken, keeping in mind the safety of the other occupants of the house, if there are any.
- If you have any pets, or your immediate neighbours have pets, be aware that the unexpected noise may be caused by an animal rather than an intruder. .

AVOIDANCE

- It is very difficult to avoid a situation when an intruder brings it into your home, but what precautions you take may make all the difference for your personal safety.
- Rubber door stops can at least delay someone from getting into the room where you have taken refuge.
- It is a good idea, if you can, to have at least two telephones in the house – one in your living room or downstairs and one in your bedroom. This way you will have two options if you need to call for help. Your mobile phone may also be available for use.

PHYSICAL

- You will have many objects within the family home that can be used to protect you:
  items from your handbag (see p. 101)
  items from your kitchen (pans can be used for hitting out or throwing, and many other items can be used very effectively given some thought) items from your bedroom (hairbrush, hairsprays, deodorants etc) items from your bathroom (sprays, perfume, deodorants, nail brushes etc)

If you think about it there are many items that can be used for protection around your home and techniques that you can use.

At all times and in whatever situation you find yourself, remember the following things:

- Any attack, whether unarmed or armed, is usually very quick or fast.
- Expect to be hurt – this will take away the fear of being hurt.
- Stay calm – if you panic, you give the attacker immediate confidence.
- Evaluate the situation – take the attacker's attitude into account.
- Take decisive action – do what you feel is necessary, but do it quickly and with confidence and intent.
- Be verbal and very loud if the situation warrants it.
- At all times be aware and remember A.P.A.P.

SITUATION: PHONE CALLS

'Funny' phone calls are usually not funny, but very upsetting, whether they are silent or verbal. You do not have to listen to them. Many people seem unable to put the phone down, but feel they must listen. Then they get very frightened, upset or distressed.

If the calls are persistent, contact your telephone company and explain to them exactly what is going on. The telephone company has several ways of dealing with this type of call. If the calls persist you can request a change of number, or go ex-directory.

If the call threatens physical violence, you must contact the police and report what has been happening. It will help the police if you have made a detailed log of all the calls – days, times and what, if anything, has been said. By doing this, when you do finally report it to the police , they can see that it is not a one-off or an isolated call. The police will liaise with the telephone company and try to locate the caller. With current technology most calls can be traced reasonably quickly.

If you feel that you would rather not go to the telephone company or the police, put a very loud whistle next to the phone. When you get an unwelcome call, give a very long and loud whistle into the phone. This is very effective in deterring or stopping unwanted calls. A hand-held foghorn will have the same effect.

If you have a telephone answering machine, then leave that on the answer mode. In this way you can listen to the caller and decide whether to answer or not. You will also have a recording of the nuisance call. Make sure that you have a few spare tapes so that you do not record over the nuisance call or calls. If you have a digital phone, you may be able to save the call.

chapter 11 in the office

Sexual harassment within the workplace seems to be on the increase, or else people are more aware of it. This section contains ways of stopping such behaviour.

The office is the most common venue for inappropriate touching or actual sexual harassment. You do not have to put up with this type of attention. The majority of men who carry out this type of harassment mean it as a joke, but it can have very serious undertones.

If such men are caught, they often say that they didn't mean it. Or it was just a silly joke. If they are not caught, they will persist until they get what they are after, or what they think they are due.

If you give into them, you may then find yourself at risk from every other male in the office as word gets around that you are fair game. Or you could find yourself with a very bad reputation. This could happen even if you refuse the attention, because most men do not like being told "NO".

If you do not comply with your attackers, they can make your place of work a very difficult place to be, and could even make things so unpleasant that you are forced out of your job, especially if the offender is in a position of authority.

There are choices you need to make, especially if the offender is in a position of authority. By retaliating against the offender, will you or could you lose your job? The choice you have to make is whether the job is worth keeping.

If you experience any type of sexual harassment that you find uncomfortable or upsetting, you must report it to your superior. Establish a record of events, so that if the situation gets really bad, those in authority can see that you have not just made it up on the spur of the moment.

If you are being harassed by your immediate superior, you must report it to their superior. There is always someone that you can go to. If you really can not go to anyone in your office or immediate workplace, report the incident, or incidents, to the personnel or human resource department. If you are not sure what to say or how to start, try something along the lines of: "I really do not want to cause trouble, but this has just happened and I feel really upset by it".

The following pages deal with a few of the most common situations that can arise in an office, but remember that many

Office parties can lead to unwelcome attention.

Most office environments are pleasant.

of the techniques can be adapted to differing situations. Most can be used deliberately (obvious retaliation) or made to look accidental ("whoops, sorry, but you were so close".).

If you have experienced any of these situations, remember how you dealt with them at the time. When you have read this section, think about how you could deal with the situation if it arose again. Although, once more, avoidance is by far the best policy. If you can feel someone getting very close, move away from them, giving yourself room to get clear or, if necessary, to retaliate.

whoops, sorry, but you were so close.

SITUATION: Standing by a photocopier, drinks machine etc

Someone standing too close

If you are standing by a photocopier, tea machine or water
fountain, there are some people who like to stand
uncomfortably close or even touching you. You can use any of
the following techniques, or a combination of the techniques.

TECHNIQUE 1

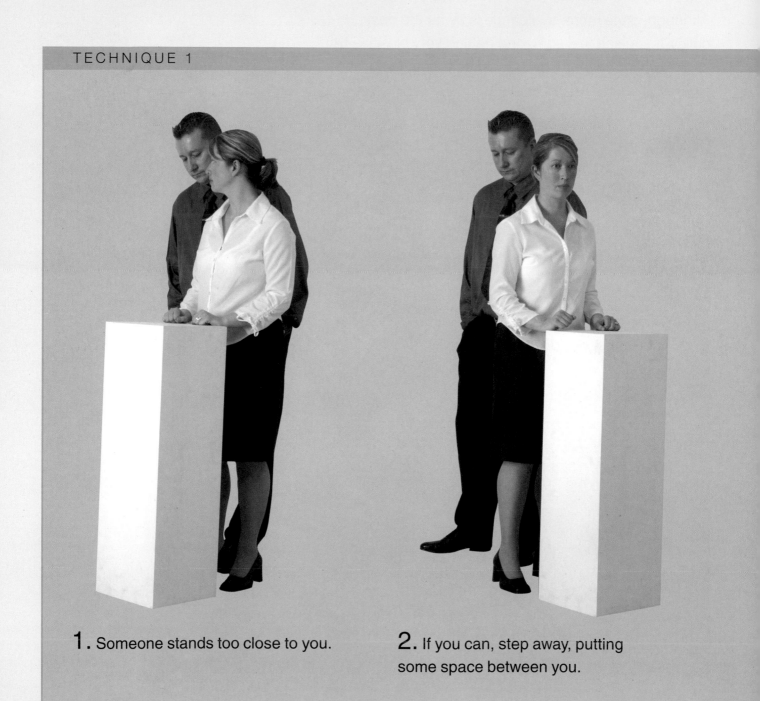

1. Someone stands too close to you.

2. If you can, step away, putting
some space between you.

3. If it is not possible to move, prepare to act.

4. Bring your elbow up, and turn your body quickly so the elbow strikes his solar plexus very hard.

Or feign surprise, and step back – very hard – onto his instep. This is very effective if you are wearing stilettos or high-heeled shoes.

TECHNIQUE 2

1. Someone comes up close behind you and puts his hand on your arm.

2. Kick back into his shin with the heel of your shoe.

If the person is so close that there is actual body contact, you can 'stumble' by pushing yourself back. Use him as a cushion should you unfortunately fall, again making sure either one or both of your elbows are slightly back.

3. You could then slide the heel down his leg and stamp on his instep. Or, just stamp on his instep.

Bracing yourself against the copier or desk, push back with a hard, sharp movement, your back hitting the person in the stomach or lower part of the body, depending on your respective heights.

Hopefully, these actions will deter the casual groper, but for the more persistent person more drastic action may be required.

TECHNIQUE 3

1. Someone comes so close that he actually touches you.

2. Place both your hands on the desk or machine.

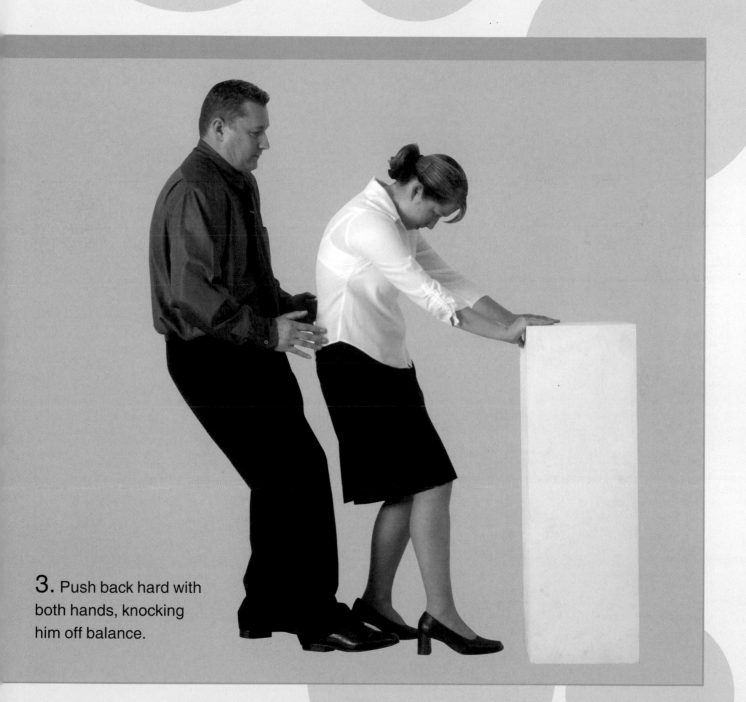

3. Push back hard with both hands, knocking him off balance.

Less subtle approaches

If someone grabs you in a more obvious manner, you may need to take much firmer action. For example, you can bring your elbow up to shoulder height and turn very quickly and strongly (using the box step on pp. 80–85), so that the elbow catches him on the neck or face, depending on your respective heights.

TECHNIQUE 1

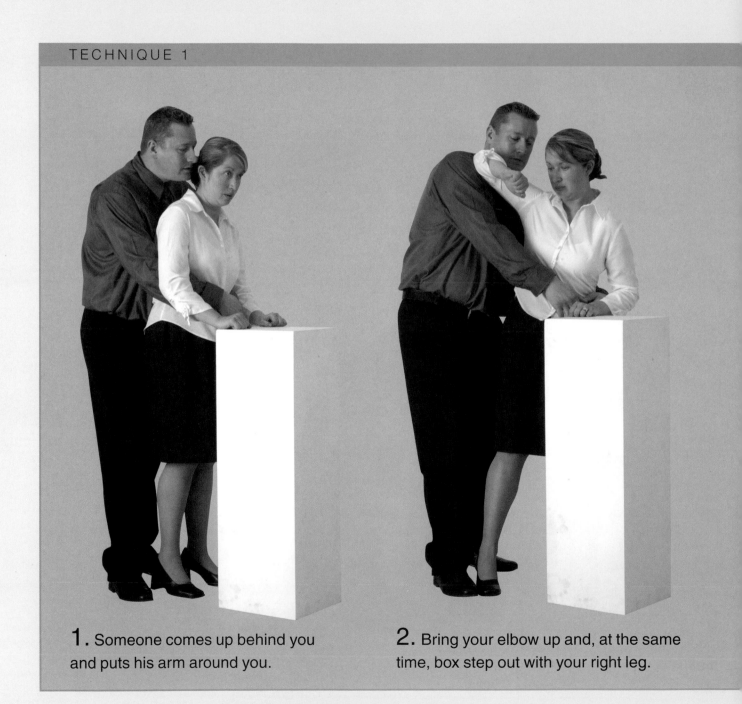

1. Someone comes up behind you and puts his arm around you.

2. Bring your elbow up and, at the same time, box step out with your right leg.

I would like to emphasise one point. If the incident, or incidents, are repeated do not use the same technique again and again. The attacker, or any onlookers, will be prepared for it, rendering the movement ineffective. Be sure to vary your techniques so that the groper or attacker will never know what is going to happen next.

3. Strike his neck or face very hard with your elbow, then move away quickly.

If someone comes up directly in front of you, again uncomfortably close, cup both hands and strike both of your attacker's ears, using a sharp, hard movement.

TECHNIQUE 2

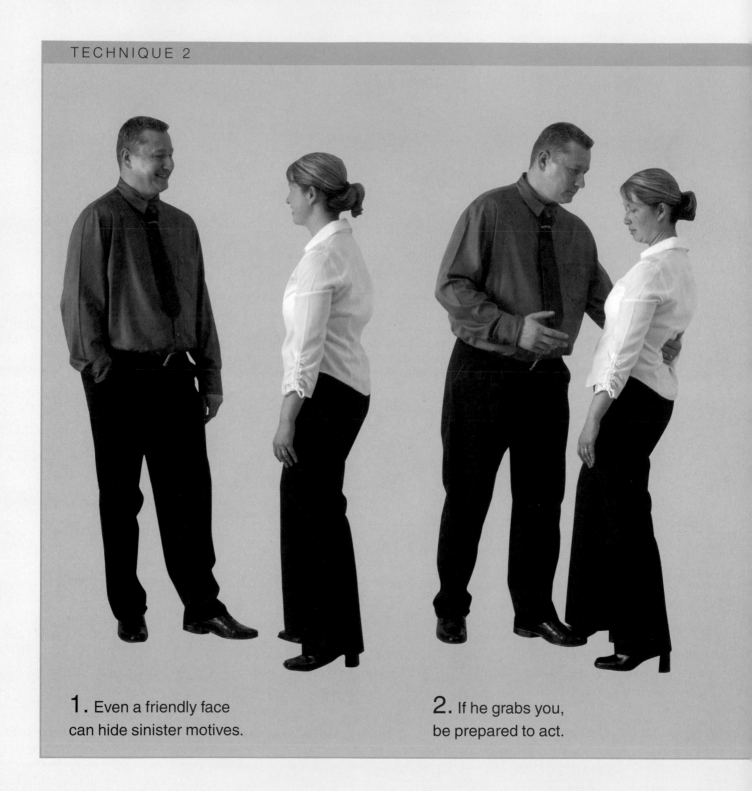

1. Even a friendly face can hide sinister motives.

2. If he grabs you, be prepared to act.

3. Bring both your hands up and cup them.

4. With a forceful movement, cup both of his ears.

Another very painful technique for your attacker is to stamp on his instep, but make sure you use the side of your foot.

TECHNIQUE 3

1. Your attacker threatens to strike you.

2. If his left leg is closest to you, do a straight kick to his knee, making sure that you use the side of your foot.

3. If your weight has moved forward slightly, you can slide your foot down his shin.

4. To finish, press or stamp down on his foot.

Or bring the heel of your hand up under his chin, pushing or striking upwards very hard.

TECHNIQUE 4

1. Your attacker tries to strike or grab you.

2. Bring your right arm up to block his left arm. Push against this arm.

3. Step forward with your left leg and, at the same time, bring your left hand up. Using the heel of the hand, strike at his chin.

4. When the heel of your hand makes contact with his chin, push your weight forwards, forcing his chin and balance back.

Sitting

If there is someone at work who likes to put his hand on your knee or thigh, the following may help to deter him.

TECHNIQUE 1

1. Someone sits very close to you.

2. Be aware of his body language.

If you have a pen, pencil or ruler, or something quite hard, such as a stapler, use it to quickly jab down into his hand.

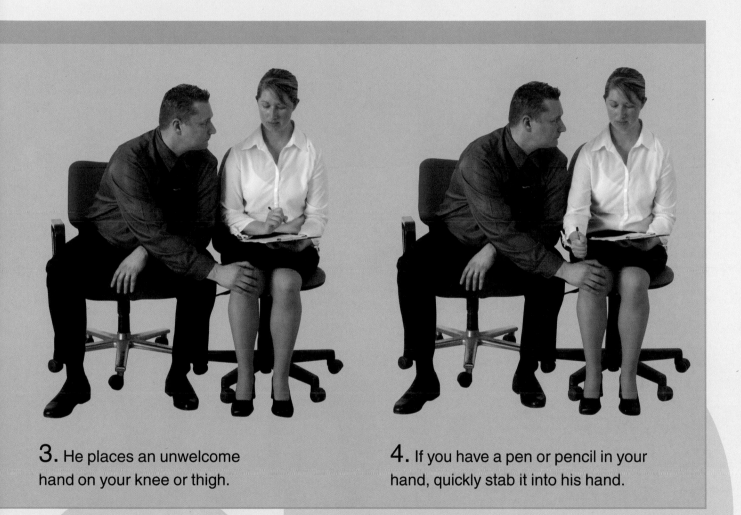

3. He places an unwelcome hand on your knee or thigh.

4. If you have a pen or pencil in your hand, quickly stab it into his hand.

If you do not have anything in your hand, try this simple technique.

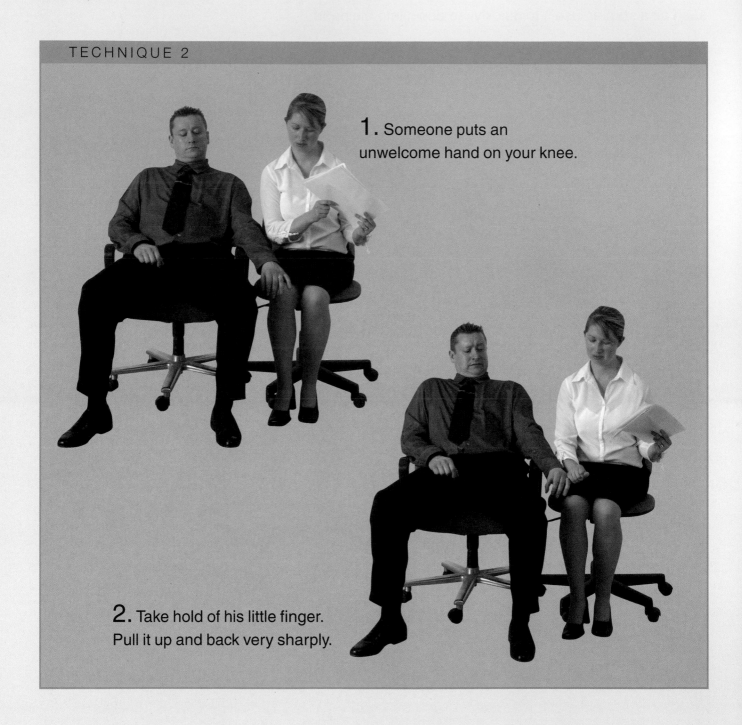

TECHNIQUE 2

1. Someone puts an unwelcome hand on your knee.

2. Take hold of his little finger. Pull it up and back very sharply.

More obvious retaliatory technique

If he puts his left hand on your thigh try this technique.

    With your left hand hold his hand and push it down on your thigh to stop any upward movement. Bring your right elbow up to the level of his face, and with a sharp movement swing the elbow back into his face.

TECHNIQUE 3

1. Be aware of body language and where his hands are.

2. When he puts a hand on your thigh, be prepared to retaliate quickly.

3. Place your left hand on his left hand and push down firmly. Raise your right elbow to the level of his face.

4. Turn your body quickly and sharply, making sure that your elbow strikes his face.

chapter 12 in closing

I have been involved with martial arts all my life, and through my own experiences and from listening to people have developed the A.P.A.P. system.

Unfortunately I cannot cover every situation you might encounter or give comprehensive advice on how to deal with them in this book. There are many techniques that would be appropriate for each and every situation you may find yourself in. All I can hope to do is offer you a guide, give you some ideas that I hope you will find helpful, and some ways to begin thinking about your safety.

I have kept the number of techniques to an absolute minimum and as simple as possible. This, I hope, will enable you to remember at least some of the self-protection techniques when you need them.

Although I hope that you never have to face an uncomfortable situation, these basic techniques can be used in many differing and varied situations. I hope that you will find them very effective.

Remember, or at least keep in mind, that although you have read this book and may have taken on board some of the techniques and ideas and although you may have practised the techniques diligently, you may not need to use them for many years. So, every now and again, you should practise them and reread the book.

It is no good if you practise them now, then forget all about them and find that in ten or so years when you need to use them, they do not work or you cannot remember them.

With all the techniques in this book, you must practise them on both sides and practise regularly. The techniques must become and remain an automatic reaction.

When in need, always contact the police, or if you are near a police station go there immediately.

If you are not close to a police station and do not see any police, use a public building to get help or phone for help.

Never go into a lonely or dark area; always stay in well lit and busy places.

Make a mental note of the attacker – height, build, colouring and any noticeable marks.

Remember every attacker has a plan, he is only looking for an opportunity. Ultimately he will be looking for someone who looks as if they will be incapable of stopping him from carrying out his plan.

If you respond with a counter attack, this may really shock him or put him off balance. Always use this reaction to your advantage by getting yourself away from the situation. Only if this is not possible, counter the attack.

In each and every situation, remember to follow the principles of A.P.A.P.

Awareness – Psychology – Avoidance – Physical

A w a r e n e s s – of your surroundings, of the people around you

P s y c h o l o g y – state of mind, remaining calm and confident

A v o i d a n c e – avoid the situation if at all possible

P h y s i c a l – if all else fails this is the last resort

If you have faced any of situations in this book, think back to how you responded at that time, and then consider how you would respond now, with the knowledge of A.P.A.P.

If you have been unfortunate enough to have been involved in such a situation, whether serious or not, and are still experiencing problems dealing with it, or you are finding that it is affecting your day-to-day life, contact your doctor or a counsellor for help. Your doctor's surgery should have a notice-board listing helpful organisations.

If you feel that you cannot go to a doctor or a counsellor, call the Samaritans or an organisation like them, and talk to someone who will be able to help you. There is a listing of helplines in your local directory or the BT directory.

No one has to suffer alone, there is always someone to help.

If you are involved in an abusive relationship, you really must get help, if not for yourself then for the other members of your family.

Useful contacts:

NSPCC Child Protection Helpline 0808 800 5000
Samaritans 08457 90 909 90
Refuge 0870 599 5443
Victim Supportline 0845 30 30 900
Rape Crisis Federation archive, www.cambridgerapecrisis.org.uk.

Contact details :
England
Wu Kung UK
email: SooWarr@aol.com

Website: www.wu-kung-federation.co.uk

America
Open Door Fitness
email : opendoorfitness@yahoo.com

INDEX

Aa

A.P.A.P. **26–55, 252**
arm around shoulders **147–9**
arm around waist **143–6**
attacks **122–138, 167–9, 172–5**
avoidance **20, 47**
awareness **15, 26–34, 58–77**

Bb

bear hug **170**
blocking **86–97**
box step **80–5**
breakdowns **112–15**

Cc

car **112–19**
car park **162–6**
cigarette **106**
comb **104**

Dd

driving **112–19**

Ff

flasher **72–3**
floor attack **132–8, 182–4**
followed **69–71, 74–5**
forward kick **130**

Hh

hairbrush **104**
handbag **101, 107–8, 201–3**
handshake **139–142**

Kk

keys **103**
knife attacks **190–211**
knife hilt, in defence **193–9**

Ll

lift **151–5**
lighter **106**

Nn

newspaper **102**
nuisance calls **222**

Oo

office **226–45**

Pp

physical **20, 47, 49, 100–9**
physical abuse **186–7**
psychology **15–16, 35–46**
punches **176–7**

Qq

questionnaire **50–5**

Rr

rape **16, 43–5, 180–5, 216**
robbery **39, 40, 118–19, 218**

Ss

sexual harassment **226–45**
side kick **129**
sprays **101**
stalked **76–7**
strike to neck **126–7**

Uu

umbrella **105, 204–7**
uppercut **128**

Ww

walking dog **156–61**

CREDITS & ACKNOWLEDGMENTS

To my father Chee Soo for giving me a good knowledge and foundation in the martial arts. Also to Grandmaster Chen Yuhe, Master Huang Jifu and Professor Li De Yin for increasing my knowledge and skills.
I would like to thank the models for giving up their valuable time to help with this book.

To my daughter Berdita and my son Jason and to Mark Colbourne (Boycee) for stepping in at the last minute.

And last, not not least, my husband Peter for his support and help

Picture credits
Pictures pp. 40, 41, 213t, 217, 222 © Getty Images
Pictures pp.14, 17, 19, 21, 22, 26, 27, 28, 30, 32, 35, 38, 42, 45, 46, 50, 57b, 59, 60, 65, 68, 70, 73, 77, 98b, 101, 102, 103, 104, 105, 106, 110, 111, 112, 113, 114, 156, 162, 181, 191, 212, 215, 219, 226, 227 © Stockbyte
(where b = bottom and t = top)